The Cambridge Manuals of Science and
Literature

# ANCIENT BABYLONIA

Silver Vase of Entemena

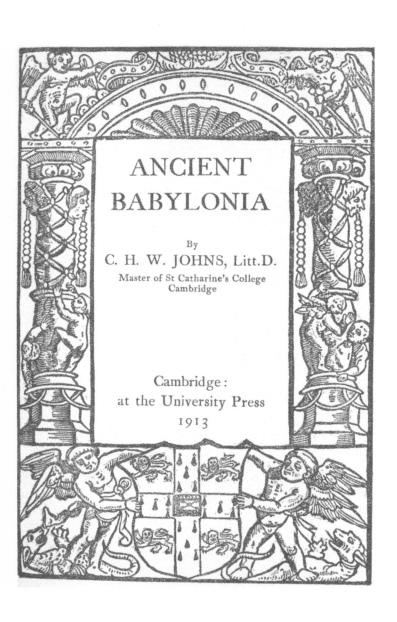

# ANCIENT BABYLONIA

By

## C. H. W. JOHNS, Litt.D.

Master of St Catharine's College
Cambridge

Cambridge:
at the University Press
1913

CAMBRIDGE UNIVERSITY PRESS
Cambridge, New York, Melbourne, Madrid, Cape Town,
Singapore, São Paulo, Delhi, Tokyo, Mexico City

Cambridge University Press
The Edinburgh Building, Cambridge CB2 8RU, UK

Published in the United States of America by Cambridge University Press, New York

www.cambridge.org
Information on this title: www.cambridge.org/9781107605725

© Cambridge University Press 1913

First published 1913
First paperback edition 2011

A catalogue record for this publication is available from the British library

ISBN 978-1-107-60572-5 Paperback

*With the exception of the coat of arms
at the foot, the design on the title page is a
reproduction of one used by the earliest known
Cambridge printer, John Siberch, 1521*

# CONTENTS

## CHAPTER I

## CHAPTER II

## CHAPTER III

## CHAPTER IV

## CHAPTER V

## CHAPTER VI

## CHAPTER VII

## CHAPTER VIII

## CHAPTER IX

## CHAPTER X

# LIST OF ILLUSTRATIONS

The frontispiece and No. I. are reproduced from *Découvertes en Chaldée* ; the remainder of the illustrations, with the exception of No. VIII., are from photographs by Messrs Mansell & Co., Nos. II.-V. being reproduced from the *Encyclopædia Britannica* (11th Edition).

# ANCIENT BABYLONIA

## CHAPTER I

### THE SOURCES OF HISTORY

THE ancient authors, who founded the Science of
History, whose names remain household words
amongst us still, such as Herodotus or Xenophon,
have transmitted to modern times some far-off
echoes of the fame of Babylonia. Many scattered
references in classical writers serve to show the
impression that its wealth and power had made on
the Greek imagination. Aeschylus and Aristophanes,
Aristotle and others, will be recalled. After
Alexander the Great had included it in his conquests, a closer acquaintance with its still marvellous
remains and magnificent traditions enhanced its
interest for many writers less generally known :
Arrian, Ctesias, Pausanias may be named.

There have been preserved some attempts on the
part of Greek-writing scribes in Babylonia to trans-
scribe Babylonian texts into Greek characters ;

doubtless with a view to studying the ancient records and rendering them available for Western peoples. We know of at least one who carried out this design. Berosus, a priest of Bêl, in Babylon, wrote a History of Babylonia, or Chaldæa, as it was then called, in three books, for the Macedonian monarch, Antiochus Soter, his patron, about 280 B.C. This work is unfortunately lost, but numerous later authors quoted extensively from it, such as Apollodorus and others. Eusebius, Josephus, Clemens and others have preserved extracts of their works. Doubtless, as cuneiform was still written in his time, Berosus, having access to much original Babylonian literature, was in a position to know many things about the history of his country, which we have not yet recovered ; but the process of transmission and the selection made by later writers leave us in some doubt as to his statements and more perplexity as to his meaning.

Before any authentic information was available, many attempts were made to collect and harmonise such references as had survived. They will be found collected in Cory's *Ancient Fragments*.

Except as the traditional home of Abraham, " the father of the faithful," Babylonia scarcely concerned the earlier writers of the Old Testament. Indeed, until the Fall of Nineveh, it played small part in the Jewish national history. The prophets have

frequent references to it, and after the Fall of
Jerusalem the home of the exiles naturally became
of absorbing interest.

Since the decipherment of the Babylonian
column of the trilingual inscription of Darius the
Great on the rocks at Behistun, by Sir H. C.
Rawlinson, Hincks, and Oppert, the native sources
have become overwhelmingly more important than
any others. Of formal or professed history little
has been recovered, for before Berosus, no
Babylonian, so far as we know, set out to write
a history of Babylonia. Of materials for history,
Babylonia has already yielded to the excavator such
an amount as to be almost unmanageable. This
short sketch can only be regarded as an attempt
to summarise, without argument or discussion, the
results now generally admitted as probable.

The Babylonian monarchs were intensely proud
of the buildings which their piety led them to
dedicate to the worship of their gods. They in-
variably left foundation records ensconced in
niches, or coffers, built into cavities in the brick-
work, at the corners, or in the floors of temples or
their annexes. These records have proved invalu-
able for identifying the buildings and the ancient
sites on which they stood. Scarcely less valuable
are the bricks of which temples and palaces were
built. For they were usually stamped or inscribed

with the name of the builder, the name of the temple or palace he had built or restored, and that of the king or god for whom it was erected.

As much information is given by the inscriptions on votive offerings, vases, mace-heads, blocks of costly stone, copper or silver vessels and other objects, often specified as the spoil brought from some conquered land. Stelæ, or monoliths, often sculptured with a figure of the king and his god, may record no more, but sometimes bear longer inscriptions. In such cases a king may name his father who preceded him on the throne, occasionally his grandfather, and even more remote ancestors. He may speak of the lands he has conquered ; but very rarely indeed draws up the annals of his reign, as Assyrian monarchs did. The Babylonian ruler apparently attached far more importance to his religious works than to any military achievements he could claim for his glory.

It may be that this reticence was the result of a long continued custom which served to commemorate the most striking event of each year in a way even more lasting than sculptured story. The Babylonians called each year by a separate name, which made a permanent record of its events, warlike or domestic. When a successful war took place the year was called after it. Of unsuccessful wars or defeats no mention was made. The Babylonian

preferred to forget them. No one could have fore-
seen a victory or the death of a foe, and it was the
thanksgiving which followed, when the spoils were
dedicated to the gods or some fresh building made
possible by them, which marked the ensuing year
as that of the victory.

The very life of the land depended on irrigation.
It was the supreme ambition of a good ruler to cut
a new canal or clean out and repair an old one.
To build afresh the city wall or its gate, to enclose a
fresh area, to build forts and palaces, often combined,
were marks of prosperity and security for its preservation. Such works often served to name the
year.

The name to be adopted for each year had to be
conferred at its beginning, on the First of Nisan,
when each king of Babylon celebrated the Feast
of the New Year's Day, and taking the hands of his
god in the temple, thus became the adopted son of
the deity and himself divine. The name of the year
being settled, all documents were dated throughout
the twelve months following by the day of the month
in the year of that selected event. Thus the names
of the first four years of the reign of Hammurabi
were (1) the year in which Hammurabi became king ;
(2) the year in which Hammurabi, the king,
established the heart of the land in righteousness ;
(3) the year in which the throne of Nannar was

made ; (4) the year in which the wall of Gagia was
built.

The name once fixed, notice of it was sent round
to the various cities or districts of the land.    These
year-names in full were often long pompous sentences
which would have been inconvenient to use in
practice.    They were usually much abbreviated.
When, for some reason, the proper year-name was
not yet known, people dated " the year after " the
last year-name.

The scribes kept records of these year-names, and
a long list of year-names has been preserved, which,
if perfect, would have given in correct chronological
order the year-names used under the First Dynasty
of Babylon from the beginning of the dynasty down
to the tenth year of the last king but one.    This
would cover  258 years.    Another such list gave the
year-names in chronological order from the twelfth
year of Dungi down to the end of his grandson's
reign ;  in all fifty-four years.

Such lists may be called Date-lists.    Such a list
of  year-names  recorded,  when  complete,  some
event, usually domestic, religious or military, for
each  year,  and  consequently  has  been  called  a
chronicle.

It is certain that the Babylonians believed that
their ancient records, based on such chronological
systems,  enabled  them  to  state  the  number  of

years which had elapsed since events long passed.

The kings of Larsa, and doubtless others before them, adopted an era. They called the years the first, second, third, up to the thirtieth, " after the capture of Isin," an event which had marked the rise of their power.

In the third dynasty, a further improvement was introduced. They then dated by the years of the king's reign. If a king died in the twentieth year of his reign, he was reckoned to have reigned twenty years. The remainder of that year was called the " beginning " of his successor's reign ; but the earliest full year after that First of Nisan, which fell next after his accession, was called his " first year." It is usual to call the fraction of a year, which fell after his accession, his " accession year," to distinguish it from this " first " year.

Presuming, which is most probable, that the royal scribes could obtain access to the necessary records, a king could state, when he desired, how long before his time an event had occurred to which he wished to refer.

Many of the later kings were not disinclined to give such chronological statements. Thus a boundary stone, dated in the fourth year of Ellil-nâdin-apli, states that from the time of Gulkishar, whom we otherwise know to have been the sixth king of the

Dynasty of the Sealand, to that of Nebuchadrezzar I.
696 years had elapsed. This dates Gulkishar about
1820 B.C. Again, Nabonidus states that he restored
a temple in Sippara, which had not been rebuilt
since Shagarakti-Shuriash, 800 years before. This
puts that monarch about 1350 B.C. Again, he glories
in having found the memorial of Narâm-Sin, who
reigned 3200 years before him. Relying on this
dating, we must place Narâm-Sin about 3750 B.C.
In another connection Nabonidus states that Hammurabi lived 700 years before Burnaburiash. This
would date Hammurabi about 2100 B.C., or perhaps
2150 B.C., according to which Burnaburiash we decide
to refer for the reckoning.

It is evident that all such dates are vague. The
numbers are only round figures, so far as we know.
Even if they be exact, we do not know from which
year of his own reign the king was reckoning, nor
to which year of the reign he quotes.

We further have a number of chronological lists
which give professedly exact chronology for certain
periods. A very early list from Nippur gives in
order the names of the kings of Ur and Isin, with the
lengths of each reign in years, even months and days.
The Chronicle of Kish gives lists of early dynasties
for some centuries, with the names of their kings and
the length of each reign.

The Babylonian Kings' List A, if complete, would

have given the names of the kings of Babylonia from the founder of the First Dynasty of Babylon down to the last native king, with the length of each reign.

The famous Canon of Ptolemy begins with Nabonassar's accession in 747 B.C., and gives the names of the succeeding kings to Nabonidus, with the length of each reign ; then the Achamenids to Alexander the Great, followed by the Ptolemies ; thus connecting with exact chronology. For Assyria, the Eponym Canon records the officials whose names dated each year, and by naming the eclipse of 763 B.C. fixes the reign of each Assyrian king back to 911 B.C. So far as they overlap, the last three sources agree exactly. Were the Kings' List A complete, we thus could trust it implicitly from the beginning. The chronology being thus more or less fixed for long periods of either Assyrian or Babylonian history, sometimes for both, except where these lists happen to have gaps, we endeavour to complete them by such synchronisms as we can discover. Kings of the one country often refer to the contemporary monarchs of the other. Naturally such a reference cannot be exact to a year.

The so-called Synchronous History dealt with the wars and subsequent rectifications of boundaries, between the territories of Assyria and Babylonia, from about 1400 B.C. to 800 B.C. Unfortunately it is not completely preserved.

The Babylonian Chronicle gave the names, lengths of reigns and some historical events of the contemporary kings of Assyria, Babylonia, and Elam, from 744 B.C. to 668 B.C.

The so-called Dynastic Chronicle had originally six columns, of which the first and second must have dealt with the mythical dynasties before and after the Flood, the third with the First Dynasty of Babylon, the fourth with those of the Sealand, of Bazu and Elam. All the rest is now lost. The names of the kings, their genealogy, length of reign, manner of death, and burial place were recorded.

Chronicle P gives some account of events from 1400 B.C. to 1250 B.C.

Chronicle K 1 deals with the reigns of Sargon of Akkad and his son, Narâm-Sin. It goes on to Dungi, Ura-imitti, Ellil-bani and Sumu-abu.

Chronicle K 2 begins with Ura-imitti and Ellil-bani, goes on with Hammurabi and Rim-sin, Samsu-iluna, Abêshu, Samsu-ditana, Kastiliash and Agum, giving selected events of these reigns.

Chronicle K 3 extended from the eleventh to the seventh century B.C., with conspicuous events of each reign.

A Religious Chronicle noted portents occurring in different years of reigns in the eleventh century B.C.

It will be obvious that such materials do constitute a reliable contribution to history, which may safely be used to construct an outline to be filled up as more material is unearthed by excavations. All the above give synchronisms, and are all in the British Museum.

The so-called boundary stones, or *kudurru* inscriptions, are records of varied kinds. They all served to rehearse a title to estate, and in doing this frequently traced it back to much earlier times, mentioning rulers or even dates.

When the system of dating by regnal years has come into use, we obtain *minimum* dates. A document being dated in the thirtieth year of a certain king, we know that he reigned *at least* thirty years, and in the absence of more exact information this hint may become valuable.

A valuable source of information is formed by the great mass of Omen tablets. The Babylonian thought that the gods not only directed human affairs, but indicated coming events by astrological signs, by the behaviour of birds and beasts, and, above all, by certain appearances to be discerned on the liver of a freshly slaughtered sheep offered in sacrifice to the gods. They reduced such augury to a science. Having observed a fancied connection of some omen or portent with an important event, they recorded both in such a way as might help to predict the events on the recurrence of the omens. From such Omen tablets we can often gather events of historical value.  We may be sure they took place, even when we cannot make out what the Omens were which were supposed to have foretold them.

In the hymns and lamentations, which formed a large part of the national literature, are frequently found references to historic events.  Even the legends have obviously, in some cases, a historic kernel of fact.

The chief cause of the many gaps still left in our history of Babylonia is the sporadic nature of the excavations.  Some sites have been exhaustively explored, but they are very few.  Several cities which were once the capitals of kingdoms, ruling over a large part of Babylonia, are still untouched by the spade ; and there, if anywhere, we must expect to find monuments of their kings.  The evidence which we now possess of their power comes from incidental references discovered elsewhere. Almost every new discovery on the sites actually being worked adds fresh proof of our existing knowledge.  But many problems must remain unsolved until other sites can be explored.

# CHAPTER II

## THE LAND AND ITS PEOPLES

BABYLONIA is, in an especial sense, the child of the two streams. The Euphrates and the Tigris both rise in the mountains of Armenia, and by the time they reach Babylonian soil have traversed a long journey. It is not easy to be sure of any natural boundary to the north, but above Hit the nature of the land is desert or rocky. There the solid ground ends in a reef of hard rock ; below, all is alluvial deposit, which now extends 550 miles down to the Persian Gulf. This is, however, greatly in excess of its ancient extent, for Eridu, once on the sea, and still an important port in the time of Dungi, is now 125 miles from the Gulf. The rivers drew within 35 miles of each other, opposite the modern Bagdad, and a little above that the Euphrates divided into two streams. The eastern branch watered the district west of Bagdad. At this part of its course, the Euphrates lies above the level of the Tigris, and a number of canals were anciently led from its eastern bank to water the extremely fertile land. The western branch, now the main stream, follows the course of an old canal, once the River of

Sippara, while the lakes and streams to the west probably mark its original course. The most important of these canals, now called the Shatt-en-Nil, empties along the Shatt-el-Kâr into the Euphrates again lower down. From the Tigris, which here is higher than the Euphrates level, the old canal, which once bore the name of the Tigris, now the Shatt-el-Hai, carries down the waters of the Tigris into the Euphrates. The Euphrates turns east below a range of low hills on the edge of the Arabian desert and joins the Tigris at Kurna to form the Shatt-el-Arab.

Ancient Babylonia lay within these rivers, which surrounded it on all sides. It formed an artificial island. While in its days of military prowess it ruled districts far outside, practically all its cities lay between the streams. In later times the northern portion was called Akkad, and the southern, Sumer. The division between them was vague, and shifted with changes in political supremacy.

The whole area was anciently a network of canals. Neglect to keep them clear led promptly to floods, as the melting snows in high lands swelled the rivers and washed away the soft earthen embankments. As the land dried up under the fierce sun, the desert sand drifted in and rendered the land a wilderness where irrigation had produced a garden. Properly managed, the district was amazingly fertile. The date-palm is indigenous, and furnished, beside food, almost endless manufactured products. Wheat was introduced early, and raised two or three crops a year, yielding 200 or 300 fold. Stone was very scarce, but excellent brick-making clay was available everywhere.

To the west of the Euphrates lay the great plain of Arabia, stretching away towards the Jordan and the Red Sea. At best bare grassland, its nomad pastoral inhabitants ever pressed down to the lands along the river and even across into the cultivated alluvial. On the east, across the Tigris, range upon range of huge limestone mountains rose to a plateau, five or six thousand feet. In the valleys, usually separated by difficult passes from each other, groups of hardy mountaineers contested with their neighbours for supremacy. From time to time they amalgamated for raids into the plain and occasionally established rule there. The invaders of upper Mesopotamia often passed down into Babylonia, and as Assyria grew into power in the north it laid claim to sovereignty over the rich southern lands.

Babylonia in historic times became a wealthy industrial land, and by its conquests absorbed multitudes of foreign slaves. Its merchants travelled far to the east for the products of Elam and Persia, even farther up the Euphrates to the

west, into Asia Minor, Palestine, and beyond to
Egypt. It was repeatedly invaded, and its conquerors infused fresh energy from time to time, but
its ancient civilisation always absorbed the invaders,
and, despite all vicissitudes, persisted in its essential
features to the end.

The remains of prehistoric peoples in Babylonia
have been met with to a considerable extent, but
are usually passed over with scanty comment. Such
of them as have reached our museums are rendered
almost worthless by an entire lack of systematic
study and scientific records. Often we do not
even know from what stratum they came.

The generations who have left no documentary
evidence of their history may be " before history "
indeed, but they were far different from " prehistoric " races, in the sense in which that term is
usually applied.

When history commences, the inhabitants of
Babylonia were already highly civilised. They
lived in towns, many of which had large populations
and occupied wide areas. They already possessed
great temples. The people had a complicated organisation of many distinct classes or occupations, and
possessed much wealth, not only in sheep and cattle,
but in manufactured goods, in gold, silver and copper.

They possessed an elaborate and efficient system of
writing, extensively used and widely understood,

consisting of a number of signs, obviously descended from a form of picture-writing, but conventionalised to an extent that usually precludes the recognition of the original pictures. This writing was made by the impression of a stylus, on blocks or cakes of fine clay, while still quite soft. These so-called "tablets" were usually sun-dried, but, in cases where preservation was specially desirable, they were baked hard. The well-baked tablet may be broken in pieces, but is impervious to moisture and, when buried in the sand, practically indestructible. The mark of the stylus looks like a hollow nail, or wedge, and hence the writing is called "cuneiform." The method was adopted by, or was common to, many of the neighbouring nations, being used freely in Elam, Armenia, and Northern Mesopotamia as far west as Cappadocia. Originally contrived to write the language of Babylonia, it was modified and adapted to express several other tongues with more or less success. We have as yet no interpretable evidence of a time before writing in Babylonia.

The art of engraving on metal and precious stones was carried to an extraordinarily high pitch of excellence at a very early date, while statuary and architecture were in an advanced stage. Pottery of excellent type and extraordinary variety was already developed. Weaving and embroidery were a staple of manufacture and export.

B

THE SUMERIANS.—By common consent this name has been given to a people who appear to have been the inhabitants of most of the cities of Babylonia, before the invasion of that land by the Semites. They are thought to have been the inventors of the cuneiform writing. Scholars differ very much as to the relation of the Sumerian to other languages, but generally agree to call it agglutinative.

Their monuments give the Sumerians a tolerably distinct physiognomy. Their fashions of dress and their characteristic customs have been much discussed, but do not appear to mark racial so much as cultural distinctions.

In early times the population of the northern part of Babylonia may have been Sumerian, and it was then called Uri or Kiuri, while the southern portion was called Kengi. Later the north, which included Agade, Sippar, Kish, Opis, Kutha, Babylon and Borsippa, was called Akkad, while the south, which included Lagash, Shuruppak, Ur, Eridu, Erech, Umma and Adab, was called Sumer.

The name Sumerian is derived from Sumer, on the assumption that the people denoted by it occupied that land where their chief monuments were first discovered.

THE SEMITES.—At what period the Semites first invaded Babylonia, when and where they first attained supremacy, are not yet matters of history.

We find Semites in the land and in possession of considerable power almost as early as we can go back.

The characteristic Semitic features are very marked on their monuments, but more decisive is the definite likeness of their language to others of the Semitic group. Apart from the modifications due to their close contact with the Sumerians, the Babylonian Semitic speech exhibits early forms of what can be traced elsewhere in other branches of the group.

They seem to have soon absorbed the Sumerian civilisation, adding elements of their own. Under their supremacy art and literature received a fresh impulse and soon attained a high-water mark.

Apparently they came into Babylonia, not directly from Arabia, but from the north-west. At any rate they first attained supremacy in the north, and Akkadian became the name of the Semitic speech. They early established themselves in parts of Elam, also in Lulubu and Gutium. Gradually they penetrated the south, and by the end of the Dynasty of Isin, Semitic was clearly understood everywhere in the land. Sumerian names lingered long in the north, much longer in the south, but we have as yet no instance of the use of the language for everyday business later than the First Dynasty of Babylon. Royal inscriptions were composed in Sumerian to the last.

THE CITIES.—BABYLON is the form which the Greeks gave to the later native name, Bâb-ilâni, " Gate of the gods " ; earlier, Bâb-ili, " Gate of god."

It lay on the E. bank of the Euphrates, part of its site being now marked by the ruins of Hillah, fifty miles S. of Bagdad. Bâbil, which preserves its name, covers the ruins of Ê-sagila, the temple of Marduk, the city god, and is still 90 feet high. The Kasr contains the ruins of Nebuchadrezzar's palace, along the E. side of which ran the sacred procession street, decorated with enamelled bricks representing the dragon and the bull, down to the Ishtar gate at the S.E. corner. The whole was enclosed within an irregular triangle formed by two lines of ramparts and the river, an area of about eight square miles. The city crossed the river to the west, where are remains of a palace of Neriglissar. The city may have become conterminous in course of time with many adjoining towns, and Herodotus ascribes to it a circuit of fifty-five miles. The *Deutsche Orientgesellschaft* have been exploring the site since 1902, and will doubtless ultimately solve the many problems afforded by it.

From very early times the kings of Babylonia wrought at the building of its temples, palaces, fortifications, bridges and quays. Hammurabi first raised it to be capital of all Babylonia. Sennacherib utterly ruined it, 689 B.C. Subsequent kings gradually restored it, but most of its ascertained remains were the work of Nebuchadrezzar. So far, the site has not yielded much material for history.

BORSIPPA.—The Greek form of Barsip, was a large city and celebrated for its great temple of Ê-zida, the shrine of the city god Nabû. The ruins of this temple and its tower are marked by the mound of Birs-Nimrud, often identified with the tower of Babel. It lay on the W. bank of the Euphrates, but Nebuchadrezzar included it in his outer fortifications of Babylon. Attempts at excavation have not yielded much. It was connected with Babylon by a long causeway and a bridge.

KISH was situated at the modern El Oheimer where have been found bricks of the great temple of Zamama, the city god. No systematic exploration has been carried out, but native diggers have unearthed quantities of tablets.

OPIS was not far away, on the W. bank of the Tigris, but the site is not identified yet. Nebuchadrezzar extended the wall of Babylon thither, thus closing the passage between the Euphrates and Tigris. Greek writers called it the Median Wall.

SIPPAR was situated at the opposite end of the Median Wall, on the Euphrates. Here have been found the site of the famous temple of the Sun-god, Shamash, called Êbarra, known to have been rebuilt by Narâm-Sin, and often restored by later kings. It was partly explored by Rassam in 1881-2, and by Scheil in 1892. Thousands of tablets were found there, of immense value for history, especially that of the First Dynasty. DEIR, close by, also yielded tablets to Budge in 1891. It probably extended beyond the modern Abu Habba.

AKKAD, the older Agade, probably lay near Sippar, but is not yet identified. KUTHA, the centre of the worship of Nergal, may be some distance N. of Kish, at Tell Ibrahim-el-Chalil, as Nebuchadrezzar seems to have included it within the Median Wall.

DÛR-KURIGALZU may have lain on the site of the great mound of Aqarqûf, on the road from Bagdad to Faluja. This has not been explored.

NIPPUR, the centre of the worship of Ellil, the Semitic Bêl, in his temple of Ê-kur, " The mountain house," was excavated for the Babylonian Expedition of the University of Pennsylvania in 1888-1895, by Haynes, Hilprecht, Fisher, and others. Its history was traced back with extraordinary completeness to the time of Sargon of Akkad. Owing to its somewhat isolated position between N. and S., and its great hold on the respect of the people, it was a repository for the votive offerings of kings both of Sumer and Akkad. Hence it has yielded more material for history than any other site. It lay at the junction of the Shatt-en-Nil and Shatt-

el-Kâr, which formed "The Euphrates of Nippur."
Not far away lies DREHEM, once the cattle-market
of Nippur, whence great numbers of tablets found
by native diggers have been exported.

At the modern Bismaya, the Expedition of the
University of Chicago, under Banks, 1903-4, discovered some of the earliest remains yet brought to
light, and proved that it was the ancient ADAB.
The site lies east of the Shatt-el-Kâr.

Still farther S. lies the modern Jokha, the ruins
of the ancient UMMA, between the Shatt-el-Hai
and the Shatt-el-Kâr. No systematic excavation
has taken place yet, but native diggers have sent
thousands of tablets to Europe. It was examined
by the Germans in 1902-3.

On the other side of the Shatt-el-Hai, and much
farther S., the mounds of the modern Telloh have
been excavated since 1877 by the French, till
1900 by De Sarzec, since then by De Cros, with
splendid results. It is the site of the ancient
SHIRPURLA, or LAGASH, one quarter of which was
called Girsu, giving the name of Ningirsu to the
city god. Owing to the thorough work done here,
we are able to reconstruct a history of the city's
fortunes as metropolis of a kingdom or under other
rule, from earliest times to the dynasty of
Larsa.

Near Telloh to the N.E., and about six miles

apart, are Surghul and El-Hibba, examined by Koldewy in 1887. Both places afforded proof that they were subject to the rulers of Lagash. Still to the south, by the Shatra marshes, Tell-Medina and Tell-Sifr yielded interesting results to a cursory examination by Loftus in 1854. Senkereh, on the Shatt-el-Kâr, was the ancient LARSA, also examined by Loftus. Many tablets from native diggings have found their way thence to Europe.

On the W. of the Shatt-el-Kâr, at Warka, are the ruins of the ancient ERECH, with the temple Ê-anna of the goddess Ninni. The mounds, covering an area six miles in circumference, were examined by Loftus in 1853. It is expected that the *Deutsche Orientgesellschaft* will shortly excavate the site.

At Fara, excavations by Koldewey in 1902 and by Andrae and Nöldeke in 1903, revealed the site of SHURUPPAK, called Shurippak in the Gilgamesh Poem or Nimrod Epos, and there described as on the Euphrates. It was the home of Utanapishtum, the Babylonian Noah, or hero of the Deluge. A cursory examination proved that a very early site had been completely destroyed by fire. Later, native diggers have sent many tablets to Europe.

Abu Hatab, somewhat farther N., was also examined by the Germans in 1902-3, and proved to be the site of KISURRA. Many tablets of the Dynasty of Ur have been found here.

Two important cities lay W. of the Euphrates by its lower course. UR was at the modern Mugayyar, where E. J. Taylor worked in 1854-5. It was the Biblical Ur-Kasdim, or "Ur of the Chaldees," whence Hebrew tradition brought Abraham to Haran and Palestine. Its enormous temple of Sin or Nannar, the Moon-god, still excites the wonder of travellers. It awaits excavation still.

ERIDU is usually identified with the modern Abu-Shahrain, situated on the edge of the Arabian desert, cut off from the Euphrates by a low pebbly sandstone ridge. Its ruins appear to rise abruptly from the bed of an inland sea. It is founded on the rock, and its buildings were of stone, not brick. Its city god was Êa, god of the deep, and tradition made it the cradle of the race.

The Babylonian city, as we first know of it, or rather as we may idealise it from the general aspect of it which we can reconstruct, was inhabited by a collection of men more or less closely allied by race, associated for purposes of mutual protection and convenience. It had its wall, within which were dwellings and buildings for stores and for folding the cattle and sheep. Outside it were meadows, irrigated from canals, and fields used to grow corn and vegetables and to produce food for the animals. An outer ring of lands was common pasture.

The city had its temple, that of the local city

god. Very obscure is still the relation of the god
to the city. He rarely bears a name which has
any relation to the city name. He may have been
the god of that tribe, which once formed the nucleus
of the city folk. Anyway, there were usually
families to whom belonged rights and duties in
connection with the temple, suggesting that they
were descendants of the founders of the temple and,
therefore, of the city.

The city, however, had long absorbed men of
other family, if not of other race, who brought
with them other gods. The religious problem, then
pre-eminently a matter of city politics, was to
cement these populations by conceding a satisfactory
place to new arrivals when they attained such power
as to demand recognition. The solution seems
usually to have been to construct a divine family.
The oldest of the gods, presumably the earliest city
god, became the father of the gods ; and the other
gods, in various ways formed the members of this
family. The theological systems thus worked out
were naturally different for each important city. A
god, once in a subordinate position, might become
in course of time far more important than other
more venerable gods.

Theoretically, the god was the owner of all the
city land, its *bêlu*, or " Lord." The inhabitants
were his tenants and owed him rent for the lands

they occupied.  The common lands were assigned
by common agreement, subject to the divine dues.
Exactly how private property in land came to exist
does not yet appear, but it would easily grow up
when the priest, who owed " the rent " for the land
he cultivated, paid it to himself as the agent of the
god who should receive it.  At any rate, we early
find evidence of its existence; it was only in
cultivated land ; pasture was common.

As the population grew by natural increase or
by the absorption of strangers, and their flocks
and herds became too great for the pastures, which
were themselves drawn upon to furnish fresh fields
reclaimed from the waste, the beasts were driven
farther afield.  Then arose disputes as to grazing
rights with the neighbouring cities.  Wars, which
seem to have been almost incessant and practically
became hereditary feuds, are early in evidence.

The aim of the successful combatant was to
preserve his own territory intact and to levy a
tribute on the conquered.  Such conquests rarely
lasted long, but gradually success fell persistently
in one direction or another, and the kings of a city
which held this loose sort of supremacy over its
neighbours form what we may call a dynasty.  It
is a dynasty of the city rather than of a family,
for the successive kings may have borne no family
relation one to another.

In spite of its submission to another city, in having to furnish a tribute in cattle, sheep, produce, corn, or goods, a quota of men to assist its sovereign in war or on public works, and an obligation not to engage in war on its own account, the subject city was autonomous. It not only kept its own city god, but made its own internal laws, exacted its own temple dues, import duties, etc.

The city governor, in whose time and through whose own energy the city became supreme over other cities, assumed the title of king. It is not clear that even when he had conquered other cities he always took this title. It does, however, seem to be the rule. When subject to the supremacy of another city, the city governor usually contented himself with the title of *patesi*. That marked him as the "steward" of his god, for whom he administered the affairs of the city, and who was the master to whom he was accountable. Even when the god had triumphed through his servants over other gods and so enabled his steward to be regarded as king over other cities, the king was still *patesi* to his own god. Hence even kings, in their inscriptions commemorating some act of religious significance, often chose to style themselves *patesi*. This title may not in such cases imply subjection to an overlord.

# CHAPTER III

IT seems probable that our earliest monuments belong to the kingdoms of the North, where Kish, Opis, Akkad, and possibly Kazallu, struggled for supremacy. We may begin there. The lack of systematic excavations at the sites of these Northern cities prevents any attempt at consecutive history. In fact, the chief witness to the existence of the Northern powers comes from records left by their invasions of the South.

It is generally agreed that the most ancient historical record we possess is preserved on three fragments of a vase of dark brown sandstone found at Nippur, below the chambers of the great temple of Ellil, on the S.E. side of the temple tower. This situation and the extremely archaic nature of the characters attest the highest antiquity. We learn that Utug, a *patesi* of Kish, son of Bazuzu, had dedicated the vase to Zamama to commemorate the conquest of Khamazi.

A colossal macehead found at Lagash was dedicated by MESILIM, king of Kish, to the city god of Lagash when Lugal-shag-engur was its *patesi*.

Êannatum, a much later *patesi* of Lagash, refers to a stele which Mesilim, king of Kish, set up to mark the boundary between Lagash and Umma.

A vase of white stalagmite, found at Nippur, close to the vase of Utug, was dedicated to the gods of Nippur by UR-ZAGE, king of Kish.

LUGAL-TARSI, an early king of Kish, is known from a small lapis lazuli tablet now in the British Museum, which records his building of a court of the temple of Anu and Ninni, probably at Erech, over which he may have ruled.

It is impossible as yet to fix the order of these, but they, like Zuzu, king of Opis, appear to have preceded that DYNASTY OF OPIS which the Chronicle of Kish puts at the commencement of its list. Here Unzi, 30 years; Undalulu, 12 years; Ursag, 6 years; Bàsha-Tsir, 20 years; Ishu-il, 24 years; and Gimil-Sin I., 7 years, form a dynasty of eight kings whose reigns lasted 99 years, when the supremacy in the North again passed to Kish. The existing copy of the Chronicle of Kish places at the head of what must be the SECOND DYNASTY OF KISH, the Queen Azag-Bau, and credits her with a reign of 100 years. She was celebrated in tradition as having ruled Sumer, and hers is the only female name ranked with the most noted rulers of Babylonia. She had been a wine seller, and founded the city of Kish according to some. Her

son, Bàsha-Sin, succeeded her and reigned 25
years. His son, Ur-Zamama, reigned 6 years.
Then Zimudar reigned 30 years ; his son, Uziwatar,
6 years ; Elmuti, 11 years ; Igul-Shamash, 11 years ;
Nanizakh, 3 years ; in all eight rulers, to whom the
Chronicle gives 586 years. The explanation of
these abnormal figures is yet unknown. Then
Kish fell under the supremacy of Lugal-zaggisi,
king of Erech, to whom we shall return.

So far as these scanty indications go we see that
at a very early period the North, under its kings
of Kish, extended its rule over the South. Lack
of material still prevents our knowing whether the
South had not earlier ruled the North. We find
independent kings almost as early in the South,
where we have contemporary evidence of their
rule and contests with the North.

Lagash furnishes records which partly overlap
the story of Kish, to which it was for a time subject.
The *patesi* of Lagash, named LUGAL-SHAG-ENGUR
on Mesilim's mace, was a subject of that king of
Kish. BADU was, however, a king of Lagash,
who certainly preceded Ur-Ninâ, and is named on
the Vulture Stele. ENKHÉGÁL, another king of
Lagash, known from an archaic limestone tablet,
may be placed about this period. The ruling
family who succeeded formed a dynasty at Lagash.

The first of them was UR-NINÂ, son of Gunidu,

and grandson of Gursar. He rebuilt the wall
of Lagash, erected temples and other buildings,
dedicated statues to his gods and cut canals to
increase the prosperity of his land. Most interesting are the plaques representing him in the capacity
of a labourer on the building of his god's temples,
accompanied by his family and court officials, or
engaged with them at ceremonial feasts. His
authority was acknowledged at Nippur and Eridu
as well as at Lagash.

AKURGAL succeeded his father, Ur-Ninâ, and
during his reign Lagash and Umma were at war.

ÊANNATUM, the son of Akurgal, succeeded him.
His magnificent Vulture Stele commemorates his
victory over Umma, which had raided the fertile
plain of Gu-edin, in the territory of Lagash. After
a fierce battle, in which Êannatum claims to have
slain 3600 men, he stormed Umma. Lagash
suffered severely, but triumphed completely. Ush,
*patesi* of Umma, probably fell in the battle, for
Êannatum concluded peace with Enakalli, a new
*patesi*. The plain of Gu-edin was ceded to Lagash,
and a deep fosse dug as a boundary between the
states. Êannatum set up a stele, with the text
of the new treaty inscribed upon it, and imposed
upon Umma a heavy tribute in grain. He was
also successful against Kish, whose king appears
upon the Vulture Stele as a captive. Elam was

*PLATE I*

Plaque of Ur-Ninâ

defeated and driven back to its own frontiers. Zuzu, king of Opis, who had invaded the territory of Lagash, was captured. Mari, a city on the Euphrates, was defeated, Ur and Erech were conquered, Larsa was in his hands, Eridu owned his rule as well as other little known but once important places. Thus Êannatum had raised Lagash to be metropolis of Babylonia. His reign was also distinguished by domestic works. He did much building at the temple of Ningirsu in Lagash and at the temple of Ninni in Erech. He further fortified Lagash, rebuilt parts of it, dug great canals, made a huge reservoir, and sank wells.

ENANNATUM I. succeeded Êannatum, whom he calls his beloved brother. Umma continued to give trouble. Enakalli was followed by Ur-lumma, his son. Each claimed the title of king. Ur-lumma destroyed with fire the stele of Êannatum and the shrines of the gods set up beside it, but Enannatum claims to have defeated him decisively. He built extensively at many temples in Lagash.

ENTEMENA, son and successor of Enannatum I., had still to defend Lagash against Ur-lumma, the king of Umma. He met and defeated him on the banks of the boundary fosse, with a loss of sixty men, followed him to Umma and slew him there. Then he annexed Umma and set an official of his own, one Ili, formerly *patesi* of Ninniesh, as ruler

c

there.  Karkar had aided Ur-lumma, so Entemena chastised it and added some of its lands to the territory of Lagash.  He erected a stela to record his victories and serve as boundary mark between Lagash and Umma.  He left memorials at Nippur, and ruled Eridu.  He further enlarged Êannatum's great reservoir, and extensively restored many temples.  His famous silver vase is the finest specimen of Sumerian metal-work yet discovered. It was dedicated for the preservation of his life to Ningirsu at Lagash while Dudu was priest there He reigned twenty-nine years.

ENANNATUM II., son and successor of Entemena, is known from an inscription upon a door socket in the great storehouse of Ningirsu at Lagash which he restored.  With him the family of Ur-Ninâ seems to have come to an end.

ENETARZI succeeded Enannatum II. as *patesi*, and reigned at least four years.  He had been chief priest of Ningirsu before he ascended the throne.  Lù-enna, a priest of the goddess Ninmar, addressed a letter to him before his accession, claiming to have defeated 600 Elamites who had raided the district of Lagash.

ENLITARZI, who had been priest of Ningirsu in Entemena's reign, succeeded, and reigned at least seven years.  He married Lùgunutur, whose steward was called Shakh.

Lugalanda-nushuga, generally called Lugalanda, was son of Enlitarzi, and married Bárnamtarra. He reigned at least nine years. Shakh continued to be royal steward in his first year, and was succeeded by Eniggal.

Urukagina, who married Shàgshàg, reigned one year as *patesi*, and at least six years as king of Lagash. The royal steward was still Eniggal. Urukagina was one of the most remarkable figures in Sumerian history. He does not seem to have been in any way related to the *patesis* who had preceded him. He ascribed his elevation to power directly to the god Ningirsu. He describes vividly the exactions of former *patesis*, priests, and officials, the oppression of the people by them, and specifies the taxes on agriculture and the swarms of collectors, spies, and predatory officials. Urukagina abolished every abuse, deprived the officials of their posts, reduced their fees, fixed fair charges, and protected the poor and weak from oppression. Restoring the conditions of earlier times he effected a grand Reformation. He also was a great temple builder and restorer, and improved the water supply of the city. He retained ascendancy over Nippur and Erech.

The reforms of Urukagina may have been important for the well-being of the people, but they undoubtedly estranged the wealthy and powerful.

Where these were in power in distant parts of the Empire—and Urukagina himself says there were "tax collectors down to the Sea," implying that his dominions extended far south—disaffection doubtless led to rebellion. Possibly also it was not easy to replace the old officials, corrupt as they were, with efficient administrators. At any rate, Lagash soon fell a prey to Umma.

How long after his accession the catastrophe fell upon Urukagina is not yet clear. A very curious tablet records that the men of Umma set fire to shrine after shrine, carried away the silver and precious stones, and shed blood in the palaces and temples. The list of the places destroyed includes all those on which the piety and wealth of the *patesis* of Lagash had been lavished. There can be little doubt that the whole city was sacked and largely destroyed by fire.

It was LUGAL-ZAGGISI, *patesi* of Umma, who simply had "wiped out" Lagash. Later *patesis* restored the city and the temples with even greater magnificence, but Lagash was never again the metropolis of the South.

DYNASTY OF ERECH.—From other sources we know that Lugal-zaggisi was son of Ukush, *patesi* of Umma. His conquests were not confined to Lagash, but he became the founder of an empire.

The chronicle of Kish informs us that he also

put an end to the dynasty founded there by Azag-Bau ; "at Erech Lugal-zaggisi reigned 25 years." Lugal-zaggisi, once *patesi*, then king of Umma, was king of Erech and of Sumer, *patesi* of Ellil, ruled over Eridu, was lord of Larsa. He boasts that he had conquered the lands from the rising of the sun to the setting of the sun, from the Lower Sea over the Euphrates and Tigris to the Upper Sea. We may, therefore, suppose that he had raided Syria, or at least received submission and tribute thence. The Chronicle of Kish only gives one king to this dynasty, and though the kings named below had probably ruled at Erech, it may well be that their power in the north was not supreme.

LUGAL-KIGUB-NIDUDU was king of Erech, Ur, and Sumer. He dedicated a rough block of diorite to Ellil in Nippur, which Shargani-sharri afterwards used as a door socket in the temple which he built there.

LUGAL-KISALSI was also king of Erech and Ur. At a later period, Gudea, when rebuilding Ê-ninnû, in Lagash, found a stele of this king and erected it in the forecourt of the temple.

ENSHAGKUSHANNA, king of Sumer, about this time successfully raided Kish, and dedicated some of his booty to Ellil in Nippur.

# CHAPTER IV

## THE DYNASTY OF AKKAD

THE absence of inscriptions from the capital of the empire ruled by this dynasty, due to the fact that its site has not yet been recognised or explored, makes our information as to the early history of the growth of power at this centre very scanty and disconnected. We may, with good reason, ascribe its rise to the energy imparted by the influx of a warlike Semitic population, but its achievements demand the assumption of much more than the incursions of a horde of fanatic warriors. The impression its power made. upon the national imagination was so striking that we must postulate a long period of prosperity for the accumulation of the necessary material resources. It cannot have owed its sudden overwhelming supremacy to a fortuitous combination of political or economic causes : it must have long awaited an opening before it marched to empire ; but only as Emperors of Babylonia do the scattered references from other sites present us with the portrait of its mighty kings, and that for the most part in long transmitted tradition of much later times. Only of recent years has contemporary evidence been available to check what seemed almost fabulous, and to separate the large element of historic truth from the myths attached to early heroes of national glory. We must await the work of the excavator for the discernment of the steps which led up to the rise of this dynasty.

The Chronicle of Kish states that " At Akkad SHARRUKÎN, the gardener, warder of the temple of Zamama, became king," after the reign of Lugal-zaggisi of Erech. Unfortunately the figures giving the length of his reign are broken away. The names of the next four kings are lost, but are plausibly restored as Manishtusu, Urumush, Narâm-Sin and Shargani-sharri. A remarkably fine monument found at Susa is engraved with sculptures which represent a battle scene and a row of captives brought into the presence of the king and his suite. The king's name is SHARRUKÎN. On the reverse, vultures are represented feeding on the slain, and a god clubbing the enemies entrammelled in his net. This conquering king is very likely the founder of the dynasty of Akkad.

Tradition has been busy with his name. As the Assyrian king, Sharrukîn II., 720-707 B.C., appears in the Bible as Sargon, it has been usual to speak of Sharrukîn as " Sargon of Akkad." The Assyrian scribes of the eighth century B.C. narrate a story of his infancy. According to this legend he was the son of a princess, a Vestal Virgin dedicated to Shamash. He never knew his father, and his father's brother ill-treated his mother, who gave birth to him in secret and confided him to the mercy of the waters in an ark pitched with pitch. He was rescued from the river by Akki, the gardener, whose craft he followed till the great goddess Ishtar made him her favourite and raised him to the throne of Akkad. His birthplace is said to have been Azupiranu.

In a collection of Omens we learn that he was " highly exalted and had no rival." He crossed over the sea in the East, and in the eleventh year subdued the whole of the Western lands, where he set up images of himself. He crossed the sea of the West in the third year and made conquests there and at Dilmun, in the Persian Gulf. He invaded Kazallu, whose king, Kashtubila, had rebelled, devastated the land, and turned the city into heaps of ruins. He made an expedition into Subartu, north of Babylonia, and defeated its people with great slaughter. In every case, he brought back great spoil to Akkad, which he made to rival Babylon. He also made a great city, like Akkad, and gave it a name, which is unfortunately not preserved, but was probably Dûr-Sharrukîn. Later, all the lands revolted against him and besieged him in Akkad. He, however, entirely subdued them, overthrew their mighty hosts, and completely re-established his supremacy.

The later tradition makes Narâm-Sin to be his son. But it is usually supposed that Manishtusu succeeded him. He married Ashlultum.

MANISHTUSU has long been known from an inscription on a mace-head found at Sippara dedicated to the goddess Ninâ. Another votive inscription found at Nippur records his reverence for Ellil. But the great monument of his reign is his famous obelisk found at Susa, written in Semitic in sixty-nine long columns. It forms a welcome contrast to the story of wars, bloodshed and spoils. It records the purchase by the king of large tracts of land near Kish, Baz, Dûr-Sin and Shittab. Each estate is described as to size, value and position, with the names of its owners and stewards. That the king bought the land of his subjects speaks highly for his respect for private ownership. Each acre of land was paid for on a fixed scale of one shekel of silver or cor of barley. Beside the price, a present of money, cattle, garments or vessels, was given to each owner bought out. A record was kept of the owner's kin who had rights of redemption over the land. The estate had given employment to 1564 labourers, under 87 overseers. The king undertook to provide fresh occupation for the displaced labourers. The men of Akkad were settled on the estate, which was destined for Mesalim, the king's son.

Two monoliths of this king found at Sippara and a duplicate found at Susa enable us to gather that when the kings of thirty-two cities combined against him he triumphed over them. That they are said to be " this side the sea " may point to his rule down to the Persian Gulf.

A number of statues of Manishtusu were discovered at Susa, carried thither by Shutraknakhunte, king of Elam, from Akkad and Ashnunnak.

An inscription on a singular cruciform object preserved in the British Museum, of which a later copy exists at Constantinople, was drawn up to record the rebuilding and endowment of the celebrated Gagîa or convent of the Shamash Vestals at Sippara. It was the work of a son of Sharrukîn, who was moved to this pious deed by the favour shown to him by Shamash when the lands left to him by his father, Sharrukîn, rebelled against him. He conquered Anshan and Kurikhum in Elam, captured their kings and brought them before Shamash.

URUMUSH, or Rimush, is known from votive vases found at Telloh, Sippara, and Nippur. One of the last is stated to be part of the spoil from Elam, which he invaded. Somewhere in that land he conquered Abalgamash, king of Barakhsu, and

*PLATE II*

Stele of Narâm-Sin

captured his viceroy, Sidqa, between Awan and
Susa, on the river Kabnitum. He sacked the city
Asharri, and "uprooted the foundations" of
Barakhsu. In this reign occurs the earliest known
bilingual Sumerian and Semitic text, recording that
Urumush had dedicated a statue of himself in lead
to Ellil. This he states to have been the first
example of its kind. From a late collection of
Omens we learn that Urumush was put to death by
a palace sedition, but no cause is assigned.

When Nabonidus laid bare the foundation inscription of NARÂM-SIN in the temple of Shamash
at Sippara, he was informed that Narâm-Sin had
reigned 3200 years before his time.

The Chronicle expressly names Narâm-Sin as son
of Sharrukîn, and states that he marched against
Apirak, constructed mines against it, took and
captured its king, Rish-Adad, as well as its governor.
He invaded Magan and took its king, Mannudannu,
captive.

From dated tablets found at Telloh we learn that
Narâm-Sin laid the foundations of the temple of
Ellil, in Nippur, and of the temple of Irnina, in the
city Ninni-esh. On his stele, found at Susa, he
records nine victories in one year. His inscriptions
record the conquest of Armânu and the capture of
Satuni, king of the Lulubu. A stele of victory was
erected by him close to Diarbekr, at the upper

affluents of the Tigris. We know the name of a
son, Binganisharri, of a granddaughter, Lipush-Iau,
and of a brother, Ubil-Ishtar.

Apparently he was succeeded by SHARGANI-
SHARRI, whose father, Itti-Ellil, may have been
an elder brother of Narâm-Sin. His existence was
first made known by the publication of a magnificent
cylinder-seal of Ibni-sharru, an official in his service.
Then a mace-head, which he dedicated to Shamash
at Sippara, was discovered. At Nippur were found
brick stamps and a door socket bearing his name, and
showing that he built at the great temple of Ellil
there.

At Telloh, De Sarzec unearthed a number of
tablets dated by events in this reign. We learn of
a successful repulse of an attack by Elam and
Zakhara upon Opis and Sakli. He reached Mount
Basar, in Amurru. He laid the foundations of temples
for Anunîtum and Amal in Babylon. He captured
Sharlak, king of Gutium. He made expeditions to
Erech and Naksu.

The same tablets bear eloquent witness to the
activity of commerce throughout the Empire. Not
only were consignments of gold and silver, herds of
oxen, flocks of small cattle, sent from Lagash to
Akkad, but grain and dates came to Lagash thence.
Lagash was in continual communication with Erech,
Umma, Ninni-esh, Adab, Nippur, Kish, and Ur.

Goods from Magan and Melukhkha on the West, and Elam on the East, slaves from Gutium and Amurru, the perpetual coming and going of messengers, or even *patesis*, from those cities, evidence a strong government and rich imports.

The Chronicle of Kish next names Abâ-ilu, followed by Ili-idinnam, Imi-ilu, Nanum-sharru, and Ilu-lugar, who together reigned 3 years. Dudu reigned 21 years, and his son, Shuqarkib, 12. The dynasty of twelve kings ruled for 197 years. Supremacy then once more shifted to the South.

The II. DYNASTY OF ERECH furnished five kings : Ur-nigin, 3 years ; Ur-ginar, 6 years ; Kudda, 6 years; Bàsha-ili, 5 years ; Ur-Shamash, 6 years; who reigned 26 years in all. As yet we have recovered none of their monuments. The dynasty at Erech fell, and the rule passed to " the army of Gutium."

CONQUEST BY GUTIUM.—Among the lamentations, which the conquest of Babylonia by the Greeks caused the inhabitants of that land to transcribe from ancient literature, doubtless as vividly expressing their own feelings at the time, is one dated in 287 B.C. It refers to the woes undergone by Babylonia at the hands of the Quti, or men of Gutium. Many cities were reduced to direst misery, described in finely poetic language. Among them are Erech, Akkad, Larak, Kharshag-kalama, Kesh, Dunnu, Nippur, Dûr-ilu, and Mash.

A date in the time of Lugal-annatum, " the year when SIUM, king of Gutium," did some great deed, may provisionally be placed here.

Whether we ought to speak of a dynasty of Gutium depends somewhat upon the length of time during which this foreign country was able to hold sway. As yet we only know of one ruler of this dynasty.

A king of Gutium, also of unknown date, called LASIRAB, has left a ceremonial mace-head, found at Sippara, and inscribed in Semitic.

Another ruler, Enrida-pizir, claims to be " king of Gutium, king of the four quarters." By its style the inscription may belong to this period, and as it was found at Nippur this king may have ruled there.

Of yet another king, by name SARATI-GUBISIN, who reigned over Umma, we may conjecture that he too was a king of Gutium, but even that is not certain.

# CHAPTER V

## LATER RULERS OF LAGASH. DYNASTIES OF UR AND ISIN

THE monuments found at Lagash give us the names of a number of rulers whose order and connection are quite uncertain. In the time of Narâm-Sin, Ur-Ê and Ur-Babbar were *patesis* of Lagash, Lugal-ushum-gal was *patesi* under Shargani-sharri, and Lugal-bur was a contemporary of the dynasty.

Palæographical considerations decide us in placing somewhat later a number of other *patesis* of Lagash, such as Bàsha-Mama, Ugme, and Ur-Mama, known from inscriptions or seals giving their names and titles. Somewhat later, UR-BAU, also *patesi* of Lagash, has left a statue and inscriptions recording the building of temples. He also constructed extensive irrigation works for the district of Gu-edin. This revival may mark the recovery from the sway of Gutium.

Ur-Bau was perhaps succeeded by Ur-gar, for whose life a daughter of Ur-Bau dedicated a female statuette. Nammakhani, *patesi* of Lagash, married Ningandu, who, with his own mother, Nin-kagina, daughter of Ka-azag, dedicated votive offerings for

his life and theirs.   Ka-azag was a *patesi* of Lagash.
Nammakhani built several temples.   Galu-Bau,
Galu-Gula, and Ur-Ninsun also were *patesis* about
this time.

The greatest of all the Lagash *patesis*, whose
power and magnificent works rival those of any
king, was GUDEA.   Under his rule it is clear that
Lagash enjoyed a considerable measure of autonomy.
His monuments are by far the most numerous and
splendid of those yet unearthed at Telloh.   His
inscriptions, placed upon twelve statues of black
diorite, on clay cylinders—two of great length, on
bricks, nails, vases, mace-heads, a lion, various
statuettes, plaques and cylinder-seals, form a great
mass of materials for the history of his reign.   They
are chiefly concerned with his great buildings.   The
magnificence with which he adorned his city is
described in a free and vivid style, and fully corro-
borated by the extensive remains already excavated.
A celebrated statue represents him as an architect,
seated with the plan of Ê-ninnû, the great temple of
Ningirsu, placed upon his knees.   For his buildings
he laid under contribution a remarkably wide range
of countries.   Cedar beams, fifty or sixty cubits
long, were brought from the Amanus range.   From
Umanu, a mountain of Menna, and from Basallu in
Amurru, he procured blocks of stone for his stelæ.
From Tidanum, a mountain in Amurru, he had

*PLATE III*

Statue of Gudea

marble sent. His copper came from Kagalad, a mountain in Kimash. From Melukha he obtained wood, and gold dust from Khakhu. Asphalt came from Madga, and fine stone from Barship on the Euphrates was carried down in great boats.

The list gives a vivid picture of the commercial connections of Lagash with Syria, Arabia, and Elam. Gudea states that his god, Ningirsu, had opened the ways for him from the Upper to the Lower Sea, *i.e.* from the Mediterranean to the Persian Gulf.

Gudea was a son-in-law of Ur-Bau.

From dated tablets we learn that Gudea was succeeded by his son, UR-NINGIRSU. He has left a ceremonial mace-head dedicated to Ningirsu, which states his father to have been Gudea, and himself to have been *patesi* of Lagash. He extensively rebuilt the temple É-ninnû and other buildings in Lagash. He reigned at least three years.

DYNASTY OF UR.—It is not clear what led Ur to disentangle itself from the debris of fallen states and gradually assume the supremacy over the whole of the South, but the enfeeblement of the older kingdoms by the invaders from Gutium and the influx of Semitic folk may well have assisted. At any rate the Semites rose to high position in the service of the Sumerian rulers.

UR-ENGUR, first king of the dynasty, reigned

D

eighteen years. Starting as king of Ur, he soon annexed Erech, Larsa, Lagash, and Nippur. At Ur he rebuilt the temple of Nannar the Moon-god, and repaired the city wall. At Erech he rebuilt the temple of Ninni and installed his own son as high priest. At Larsa he rebuilt the temple of the Sun-god. At Nippur he rebuilt the great temple of Ellil. At Lagash he dug a canal in honour of Nannar of Ur to serve as a boundary ditch. He claims to have administered justice in accordance with the laws of Shamash. So far his reign was peacefully employed in gathering resources and consolidation. One note of aggression lies in the year-name, "in which Ur-Engur the king went from the lower to the upper country." It may point to a royal progress to receive the submission of the North, or may hint at conquest.

DUNGI, son of Ur-Engur, succeeded him on the throne. A late Babylonian Chronicle states that Dungi sacked Babylon and carried off the treasures of É-sagila. This event may have fallen before his thirteenth year. The Date-list will furnish the skeleton of his annals. In the thirteenth year the foundation of the temple of Ninib was laid, probably in Nippur. In his sixteenth the procession Bark of Ninlil, goddess of Nippur, was repaired. In his seventeenth year Dungi installed Nannar in his temple at Karzida, near Nippur. Next year a royal palace seems to have been completed. So far Dungi appears to have chiefly concerned him self with Nippur. In his nineteenth year, Kadi, the city god of Dûr-ilu, was installed in his temple there. Next year the city god of Kazallu was similarly restored to his temple. In his twenty-first year another royal residence was completed. Next year Nannar of Nippur was installed in his temple. In his twenty-third year the high priest of Anna was designated by an oracle to be high priest of Nannar in Nippur. Thus Dungi united in his own person two of the highest priestly dignities in the land. In his twenty-fourth year the nuptial couch for Ninlil, goddess of Nippur, was constructed, and next year Dungi became high priest of Ur, thus carrying on his policy of centralisation. In his twenty-sixth a very remarkable step was taken. Dungi's daughter, Niugmidashu, was exalted to be lady of Markhashi. This district is thought to have lain in Elam, but may be Mar'ash, in Northern Syria. She is apparently sole ruler over her district. Next year the city Ubara was restored. The date of the twenty-eighth year records that the men of Ur were enrolled as long-bow archers. In the twenty-ninth year the god Ninib became *patesi* of Ellil. Although Nippur had its *patesis* in the early part of the reign, it was a stroke of genius to replace

the human *patesi* by the war-god Ninib. Next
year Ellil and Ninlil were again honoured.

So far we have watched Dungi's masterly policy
of consolidation and conciliation. Now, secure at
home, he set out on a career of conquest. In his
thirty-fourth year Gankhar, in Elam, was raided.
Next year Simurum was attacked and again the
year after. Kharshi was raided in his thirty-seventh
year. Then Dungi was made High Priest of Eridu.

In the Babylonian Chronicle K 1 we are told that
Dungi cared greatly for Eridu, which still lay on
the sea. His own inscriptions mention his building at the temple of Enki there.

Again Dungi turned his attention to Elam. In
his fortieth year the *patesi* of Anshan married the
king's daughter. Next year Gankhar was raided
again. The attack was repeated next year, and
Simurum was raided a third time. In the. forty-
fourth year Anshan was raided. In the forty-
sixth year Nannar of Karzida was installed the
second time. Dungi next built the wall Bàd-
mada. In the forty-ninth a temple of Dagan was
built, possibly at Drehem, the chief cattle-market
of Nippur.

After this period of recuperation Dungi raided
Shashru, in Elam, in the fifty-second year. Next
year the Crown Prince was the High Priest of
Nannar. In the fifty-fourth year Simurum and

Lulubum were raided for the ninth time. Next year Urbillum was raided, and with it Simurum, Lulubum, and Gankhar were again attacked. In the fifty-sixth year Kimash, Khumurti and their lands were ravaged. No new event is recorded next year, but in the fifty-eighth year Kharshi, Khumurti, and Kimash were raided.

From his own inscriptions we learn further that he was a great builder. The temple of Nergal at Kutha, the temple of Ninni at Erech, the temple of Nannar at Ur, were rebuilt or enlarged by him. The great wall of Erech, two royal palaces at Ur, the temple at Lagash, and temples of Ninâ and Nin-mar there were built. He introduced standards of weight ; examples have been found which state that they had been tested in the weigh-house of Nannar at Ur, in his time.

Bûr-Sin, Gimil-Ellil, Nadi and Ursin are known as his sons, and two daughters, Shat-Sin and Niug-midashu.

Dungi was succeeded by his son, Bûr-Sin I., who reigned nine years. In his second year he raided Urbillum. In his third year he honoured Nippur by making a great throne for Ellil. Next year the exalted High Priest of Anna, Bûr-Sin, was invested High Priest of Nannar, and the year following High Priest of the great Sanctuary of Innina. In his sixth year Shashru was raided,

in the seventh year Khukhnuri was raided. Next
year Bûr-Sin was made High Priest of Eridu, and
the year following High Priest of Nannar of
Karzida.

From his own inscriptions we know that he added
to the great temple Êkur in Nippur, built a storehouse there, added to the temple of Nannar at Ur,
improved that of Enki at Eridu, and rebuilt part
of the temple of Ninni at Erech. His reign over
Susa is attested by documents dated in his reign.
From Drehem we learn that in his fourth year he
had raided Shashru and Shurutkhu, and in his
seventh destroyed the cities Bibrabium and
Jabrum.

Gimil-Sin, Gimil-Ishtar, and Dungi-rama were
his sons.

GIMIL-SIN II., his son, succeeded Bûr-Sin, and
reigned nine years. In his second year the Bark
of the " Antelope of the Deep," a title of Enki of
Eridu, was made. Next year he raided Simanum,
in Elam. In his fourth year he built the Bàd-
Martu, or " Wall of the West," called Muriq-Tidnim
or " Warden of the Tidnim." In his sixth year
a great stela was erected to the honour of Ellil.
In the seventh year the land of Zabshali was raided.
We also know that during this dynasty the daughter
of the king of Ur, called Tukîn-khatti-migrisha,
married a *patesi* of Zabshali. Next year a great

bark was built for Ellil and Ninlil. In the ninth
year he built a temple for the city god of Umma.
From his own inscriptions we further learn that he
built a temple for Nannar at Ur. Lugal-màgurri,
*patesi* of Ur and commander of its fortress, built
a temple there for the worship of Gimil-Sin himself.
A brick of his was found at Susa.

Gimil-Sin was succeeded by his son, IBI-SIN,
who reigned twenty-five years. An Omen tablet
states that he was carried captive to Anshan. We
may conclude that an Elamite invasion put an end
to the dynasty of Ur. It may have been the same
invasion as that in which Kudur-nankhundi, king
of Elam, carried off the image of the goddess Nanâ
from Erech, which Ashur-banipal restored after
his capture of Susa about 650 B.C. The Assyrian
king reckoned that it had been captive for 1635
years. This would place the fall of this Dynasty
of Ur 2285 B.C. From dated documents we know
that Ibi-Sin had raided Elam, attacking Simurum.

IBI-SIN left a son, Nitamu, but the supremacy
passed to Isin after his father's death, and he never
reigned. We also know of Ur-Ninsun, Nabi-Sin,
and Nabi-Ellil as king's sons, but not which king
was father of any one of them.

The thousands of commercial documents, temple
accounts, cylinder-seals, and smaller inscriptions
from the ancient cities of Lagash, Umma, Nippur,

Drehem, and far off Susa, which have been edited
of late years, throw considerable light upon the
extent of territory ruled by the kings of Ur at this
period.   Most of the cities under their rule were
governed by *patesis*, and we have recovered the
names of many of these rulers.   As the list
approaches completion we may obtain data for
marking the spread of Semitic influence.   Far from
the  population  being  predominently  Sumerian
in the South, we witness the rise of Semites to the
highest offices, even in the very homes of Sumerian
culture and language.

A  most  striking  example  is  WARAD-NANNAR,
who, as early as the fifty-seventh year of Dungi,
was *sukkal-makh*, or  Grand  Vizier  and  *patesi*  of
Lagash.   His own Semitic inscriptions state that
he also became priest of Enki at Eridu ; viceroy of
Uzargashana, Bashime, Timat-Ellil, Urbillum, and
Nishar ; *patesi*  of  Sabum, Al-Gimil-Sin, Hannab
and Gankhar ; regent of the Sû folk and of Kardaka,
but still the humble servant of Gimil-Sin.   At Lagash
he built largely at the temple of Girsu.   His power
lasted into the third year of Ibi-Sin.   His father,
Urdunpaè, and his grandfather, Lani, both Sumerians, had been Grand Viziers before him, as he
was under four kings of the dynasty.   He claimed
to have conquered Khamazi.

These  documents  further  show  the  perpetual

interchange of products and goods between the cities of the Empire down to Dilmun in the Persian Gulf and up to Mari, high on the Euphrates. The so-called Cappadocian tablets, about which so many speculations have been indulged, prove to be dated in the reign of Ibi-Sin, king of Ur. The language then written, and probably also spoken, in Cappadocia was Semitic Babylonian. The style of writing persisted there till it was adopted by the Hittites of the fifteenth century B.C., and used in their correspondence with Assyria, Babylonia, and Egypt. We have then to conclude that the kings of Ur not only fetched cedar and other products from the Lebanon, but ruled far into Asia Minor itself.

DYNASTY OF ISIN.—Isin is frequently mentioned as subject to the kings of Ur ; and it probably suffered the same fate. The revival of power after the Elamite invasion is marked by the rise of a new dynasty, largely Semitic in its complexion. We have seen reason to suspect that the ruling class in Elam was now largely Semitic.

The dynastic list from Nippur gives the dynasty of Isin as sixteen kings who reigned in all 225 years. Their bond of union is that Isin continued to be the capital for that period, but there were at least two breaks in the succession.

The first king, ISHBI-URRA, reigned thirty-two

years. An Omen text speaks of him as " a king
without rivals." His son, GIMIL-ILISHU, reigned
ten years. IDIN-DAGAN, his son, reigned twenty-
one years. A fragmentary inscription found at
Sippara suggests that his rule included the North.
A contemporary hymn shows that he built at
Nippur. Another hymn from Sippara is addressed
to him as a god. His son, ISHME-DAGAN, succeeded,
and reigned twenty years. A brick found at Ur
gives his titles as King of Isin, Sumer and Akkad,
Lord of Erech, benefactor of Ur, Nippur and Eridu.
Numerous bricks found at Nippur attest his buildings there. LIBIT-ISHTAR, his son, reigned eleven
years and bore the same titles as his father.

In the time of Libit-Ishtar, or on his death, Ur
appears to have thrown off the yoke of Isin and
combined with Larsa to form an independent
kingdom. A brother of his, Enannatum III.,
High Priest of Sin at Ur, for the preservation of
his life and that of GUNGUNU, king of Ur, rebuilt
the temple of Shamash at Larsa, doubtless destroyed in the Elamite invasion. Now Gungunu
himself rebuilt the great wall of Larsa, and claimed
to be king of Larsa, Sumer, and Akkad. At this
time Isin must have ceased to be capital of Babylonia. The death of Gungunu is used to date a
tablet from Larsa. It was long believed that
Gungunu preceded Ur-Engur, and hence that ruler's

dynasty was called the second dynasty of Ur.
Another early king of Ur, SUMU-ILU, may have
reigned about this time. Abba-dugga, son of
Urukagina II., dedicated a steatite dog to the
goddess of Isin for Sumu-ilu's life. The name of
Sumu-ilu suggests Amorite affinities.

The dynastic list, however, does not name either
Gungunu or Sumu-ilu, but passes directly to the
next king of Isin, without at all suggesting any
interval. UR-NINIB, whom it names next, reigned
twenty-eight years. He does not seem to have
been related to the family which had governed Isin
for ninety-four years. He claims to be king of Isin,
Sumer and Akkad, Lord of Erech, benefactor of
Nippur, Ur and Eridu. He had then won back his
predecessors' kingdom. His son, BÛR-SIN II.,
succeeded him, and reigned twenty-one years, with
the same titles as his father. He built the wall
of Isin. His son, ITÊR-BÀSHA succeeded, and
reigned five years. He seems to have died without
issue, for his brother, URRA-IMITTI, succeeded him,
and reigned seven years. A late Babylonian
Chronicle K 1 relates that, having no issue, he
nominated Ellil-bani, his gardener, to succeed him.
After placing the crown on Ellil-bani's head, he
died an obscure death, whether by accident or
treachery is not clear. In the History of Agathias
the story is told of Beleous and Beletaras, supposed

to be Assyrian kings. SIN-IKISHA disputed the succession, and held the throne for six months. He named one year as that in which he made an image of gold and silver for Shamash. ELLIL-BANI, " the gardener," succeeded after Sin-ikisha's suppression, and reigned twenty-four years. An inscription of his puts his benefits to Nippur in the first place, which, as well as his name, suggests a connection with that city. His titles imply rule over Isin, Sumer and Akkad, Erech, Nippur and Ur. He built a great wall at Isin, called after himself.

The next king, ZAMBIA, reigned for three years, but apparently was no connection of Ellil-bani's. Two kings followed, whose names are not yet recovered with certainty, and reigned five and four years respectively.

SIN-MAGIR reigned eleven years. He ruled over Babylon, where he dedicated a votive offering. He was king of Isin, Sumer and Akkad. Some think that his omission of Ur was due to the fact that it had again become independent under Sumu-ilu.

DAMKI-ILISHU I., his son, reigned twenty-three years. Damki-ilishu built a wall of Isin, and his rule was perhaps acknowledged in Sippara. He also built the temple of Shamash in Babylon, and ruled at Nippur. At any rate, in the beginning of his reign, he still ruled both North and South Babylonia, and claimed to be king of Sumer and Akkad. Simmash-shipak later claimed descent from him.

The capture of Isin by Sin-muballit in his seventeenth year is thought by some to have put an end to this dynasty. Rîm-Sin, king of Larsa, also captured Isin, and his capture was so noteworthy that an era was dated by it. Assuming that the end of the Isin era of thirty years coincided with the thirty-first year of Hammurabi, Isin may have fallen as a dynasty about the beginning of his reign. The question, however, is still most obscure ; and the end of this dynasty may really have preceded the rise of the First Dynasty of Babylon.

THE AMORITES, or Amurrû people as they called themselves, were a branch of the West Semites, who had for a long time been settling in Babylonia. It is generally believed that they had already possessed themselves of great parts of Syria and Palestine, where Hebrew tradition records their presence. It is by no means certain that those who settled in Babylonia arrived there from the West through Mesopotamia. They may have been a branch who came into Babylonia while their brethren settled in the West. At any rate Hebrew tradition represents Abraham as migrating from Babylonia to the West, doubtless under pressure of the Elamite invasion of the South.

It was in the North that the Amorites succeeded

in gaining supremacy, and infused such energy as to lead to the rise of the powerful empire of Babylon over both Sumer and Akkad. It is clear that the Amorites had made a great impression on the South under the kings of Ur and Isin, if they did not actually furnish several kings of the latter dynasty. But in the North the Semite was already predominant, and fusion was more immediate and complete.

Before the rise to power of the First Dynasty of Babylon, affairs in the North had been very unsettled. Perhaps the triumphs of the South had weakened the city states, and when the Elamite invasion broke the power of Isin and placed the sons of Kudur-Mabug on the throne of Larsa, the North was no longer united by a strong over-lord. At any rate we find independent kings at Kish and Sippara contemporary with the first kings of Babylon, Sumu-abu and Sumu-la-ilu. We cannot yet disentangle the chronology, but starting with Kish we note the rise of Amorites there.

ASHDÛNI-ERIM, king of Kish, has left a small clay cone, now in the Louvre, written in Semitic, which narrates that when the four quarters of the world revolted, he fought without success against the enemies for eight years until his own army was reduced to 300 men. Then Zamama, his lord, and Ninni, his lady, came to his succour, and in forty days he subdued the land of the foe. Then he rebuilt the great wall of Kish. We may assume that he had succeeded to a wide kingdom, but except by style and script we cannot date him, nor do we know who was his obstinate foe. Possibly the Amorite invaders, possibly Rîm-Anum ; and he may be even earlier.

A THIRD DYNASTY OF KISH overlapped the First Dynasty of Babylon. At present only a few kings are known, and they only from contracts dated at Kish in their reigns. When they use the same year-names as Sumu-abu or Sumu-la-ilu we may suppose them vassals of these kings of Babylon, but when they use dates commemorating their own deeds, they surely claimed independence. They may be subject to the kings of Kazallu.

KHALIUM dug the canal Mê-Ellil, and reigned at least three years before Sumu-abu's third year.

SUMU-DITANA built the walls of Mà and Karash, and reigned at least three years. A later king, Japium, records his death, so probably he was deposed.

MANANÂ used his own dates for seven years. He came to the throne later than the third year of Sumu-abu, and made a tambourine or drum for the temple of Nannar of Ur, whose worship seems to have been imported into Kish. He also honoured Shamash, and set up a great bronze statue

of himself. Later he uses a dating which ascribes
the conquest of Kazallu to Sumu-abu. This
took place in that king's thirteenth year when
Mananâ must have been an ally or vassal. As his
name occurs as co-regent with Japium that king
must have immediately succeeded him.

JAPIUM set up a bronze statue of himself, dedicated a crown for his god, dug a canal for Kish,
made a tambourine for Zamama, each in a separate
year, and chose his own dates for nine years at
least. He reigned still as a vassal in the fifth year
of Sumu-la-ilu, who captured Kish in his thirteenth
year. ALISADU appears to have ruled along with
him at the end of his reign, and so may be his immediate successor. MANIUM was also one of the
kings of this dynasty, but it is not possible yet to
assign him a position. It was long ago pointed
out that several kings, reigning at Sippara, were
contemporaries of the kings of the First Dynasty
of Babylon.

BUNUTAKHTUNILA bore the title of king and used
his own date formula at one time. Later he is
associated with Sumu-la-ilu as ally or vassal.

IMMERUM was also associated with Sumu-la-ilu.
Yet he used his own dates, from which we learn
that he honoured Shamash and dug the Ashukhu
canal. He has been identified with Nûr-Adad of
Larsa, but this can hardly be the case.

ILU-MA-ILA I. was a contemporary of both Sumu-la-ilu and his son, Apil-Sin. He seems to have been a mere puppet, and must not be confused with the first king of the Sealand.

NARÂM-SIN II. ruled about this period, probably independently, and built a shrine for his god ; but it is still impossible to assign him a date.

MANABALTEL also ruled some city in the North about this time, but no more is known of him.

In the South we have an equally difficult task to arrange the rulers before the First Dynasty extended its sway over that area.

RÎM-ANUM reigned at least eight years as a great conqueror. In one year-name he commemorates the capture of Erech and its people ; in another that of Emutbalum : on a tablet, for long the only record of his existence, he enumerates his conquests as Emutbalum, Ashnunnak, Isin, and Kazallu. The text, written in Sumerian, may be only a year-name, but it would be a surprising record of conquest for one year. Many tablets dated in his reign are concerned with slaves, obviously captives in war. Many of these were Asiru, who bear West Semitic names and were under a separate overseer. These people also appear in inscriptions of Sin-muballit, and Pukhia, king of Khurshitu, near the Aksu, a tributary of the Adhem, was of their race. The Amurrû also often occur

E

and had a separate overseer. The captives came from Babylon, Isin, Sarabi, Sûrî, Ashnunnak, Gutium, Sippar, Kar-Shamash, Larsa, Ê-abba, Karab, Kisurra, and Kish. Some of the slaves he retained, others were sent back to their homes. We must regard him then as a great conqueror, and there is not room for his operations after the First Dynasty came into power. The records all come from Kish, where he certainly ruled, but which of the cities above enumerated was his capital does not appear.

A number of kings ruled at Larsa and Ur. We have noticed Gungunum and Sumu-ilu.

The explorations of W. K. Loftus in 1853 at the mounds of Warka, the ancient Erech, and at Senkereh, the ancient Larsa, have been already noted. He sent a few workmen across the Shatt-el-Kâr to explore the mounds of Tell-Sifr. They discovered over a hundred well-preserved unbaked clay tablets, now in the British Museum. Being still in their clay envelopes these excited great interest at the time. They were dated in the reigns of Hammurabi, Samsu-iluna, Rîm-Sin, Nûr-Adad and Sin-idinnam. They were records of the business of one family which grew from small beginnings to be large estate owners. These kings must therefore be closely related in date. Some of them have left monuments of their own. These so-called

Warka tablets have proved most valuable material for history. They fix the following sequence of kings :—

Nûr-adad, on a votive cone, calls himself king of Larsa and shepherd of Ur. He built an annex to the great temple of the Moon-god at Ur. He further made a throne for Shamash at Larsa, and reigned at least five years. His son gives him the title king of Sumer and Akkad.

Sin-idinnam, his son, succeeded as king of Larsa, Sumer and Akkad. He claimed rule over Ur. He dug out the Tigris canal, built Dûr-gurgurri, a great fortress on it. He boasted of his victory over all his foes ; built temples at Larsa, Ur, Adab ; and a great wall at Mashgan-shabri. He reigned at least six years. No long interval can have separated his reign from that of Rîm-Sin.

Kudur-Mabug, son of Shimti-Shilkhak, who both bear Elamite names, calls himself " overseer of the Amurrû." It is clear that an Elamite invasion had placed this ruler of Emutbalum, once conquered by Rîm-Anum, over the whole South. He claims to have rebuilt at Ur the same annex of the Moon-god temple which Nûr-Adad had erected. This was done for his own life and for that of Warad-Sin, his son, whom he calls king of Larsa.

Warad-Sin himself adopts the old style of Nûr

Adad and Sin-idinnam, "king of Larsa, king of Sumer and Akkad who cares for Ur." While his father seems to have retired to his ancestral domains, Warad-Sin built a great wall at Ur, temples at Nippur, Ur, Larsa, Eridu, Girsu, Lagash, Khallab and other cities, usually for his father's life as well as his own. He must have reigned at least four years. He may be the Eri-aku of the Kudurlakhamar Legends and the Biblical Arioch of Genesis xiv.

Rîm-Sin was also son of Kudur-Mabug and brother of Warad-Sin. In his early inscriptions he speaks of his father as still alive. He was then prince of Nippur, protector of Ur, king of Larsa, king of Sumer and Akkad, while his father was ruler of Emutbalum. He soon was able to extend his power. Sin-muballit, in his fourteenth year, defeated the army of Ur, doubtless led by Rîm-Sin, and in his seventeenth year captured the city of Isin. Here he probably left Damki-ilishu, the last king of the Isin dynasty, as a vassal. Soon after, perhaps at Sin-muballit's death, Rîm-Sin was able to capture Isin, and for a long while, thirty years at least, the South of Babylonia continued to date by anniversaries of its fall. His rule was acknowledged at Larsa, Lagash, Nippur, Erech, in this period. Hammurabi does not seem to have crossed swords with Rîm-Sin all this while, but in

*PLATE IV*

**Votive Figure of Warad-Sin**

his thirtieth year Hammurabi repelled an Elamite attack. Whether Rîm-Sin sided with the Elamites or was weakened by them is not clear, but next year Hammurabi signally defeated Rîm-Sin, whom he styles simply king of Emutbalum. Gradually the whole of Rîm-Sin's dominions fell into the hands of Hammurabi. Samsu-iluna retained possession of the South till his eighth year, but the invasion of Babylonia by the Kassites next year evidently gave Rîm-Sin an opportunity of which he made good use. In his tenth year Samsu-iluna defeated Rîm-Sin and his allies, the Idamaraz, capturing Emutbalum as well as Erech and Isin. According to Chronicle K 1, Samsu-iluna put Rîm-Sin to death at this time. Many identify Rîm-Sin with Arioch.

Beside his Isin era of thirty years Rîm-Sin used the old method of dating for at least eight years, one or two of which fall after the eighth year of Samsu-iluna, but six must fall before the reign of Hammurabi. He can hardly then have reigned less than fifty-nine years in all. These year-names cannot be arranged chronologically with any certainty. He dug out the Euphrates bed, doubtless near Nippur, to the South. He cleared the course of the Tigris, or possibly the Shatt-el-Hai, down to the sea coast. He brought into the temple of the Sun-god at Larsa two bronze images representing himself in the attitude of worship. He restored

the temple of Ea at Ur. He further dug a canal
at Nippur. These five events probably mark five
years before the conquest of Isin. The year when
he smote down with his mace the army of Erech,
the year when he captured Kisurra and destroyed
Dûr-ilu, and the year when he captured Nazarum
and destroyed the walls of Asida may belong to
the revival of his power in the South, but more
likely to his earlier campaigns. During his power
in the South he was an active restorer of temples
and city walls. He married Simti-Ninni, daughter
of Warad-Nannar.

We have passed in review the kingdoms which
were partly contemporary with the great First
Dynasty of Babylon, to which we now turn as the
rival that finally conquered and absorbed them all.
So doing it came in contact with the rising power
of the Sealand kings, whom we shall meet later.

Although these kings of the South had arrogated
to themselves the proud title of kings of Sumer and
Akkad, the latter was clearly an empty title, since
Rîm-Anum's time, for there can have been little
power in their hands in the North.

# CHAPTER VI

## THE FIRST DYNASTY OF BABYLON

THIS name was early given, because the Babylonian
Lists of Kings began with this dynasty, and it was
there described as " of Babylon." The lists of
year-names, as well as the Kings' Lists, attest the
presence at its head of one SUMU-ABUM, whom we
may regard as having founded the dynasty. While
the throne descended from father to son after him,
the later kings merely claim descent from his
successor, Sumu-la-ilu, and that king appears to
have been no relation of his.

If Sumu-abum was the victorious chief of an
invading swarm of Amorites we have as yet no
record of his conquest of Babylon. We know
nothing of the kings of Babylon who preceded him.
We have seen that men of his own race had formed
a kingdom at Kish, and with them he warred. It
seems that in a still obscure period the Amorites had
swarmed into Northern Babylonia, deposed the
local princes, sporadically founded new dynasties.
Among these, Sumu-abum, by his own talents or
by the larger number of Amorites under command,
forced Babylon into predominance over its neigh-

bours.   How far the resources it already possessed
had fitted it for this position, we do not know.

It is practically certain that Babylon did not
become the metropolis of the empire by accident,
nor did the Amorite dynasty arise by magic, but
the history which explains its rise is as yet without
record, and we must take up the story where we can
read it in the inscriptions that have come down to
us.

We are almost entirely dependent upon the date
list for our knowledge of SUMU-ABUM's reign.   From
Chronicle K 1 we learn that Sumu-abum warred
with Ilu-shumma, king of Assyria.

In his third year he built the wall of the city
Kibalbarru, near Babylon.   Next year the temple
of Ninisinna was built there.   Next year a temple of
Nannar was built, probably in Babylon.   In the eighth
year a great door of cedar was made for this temple.

In his ninth year the wall of Dilbat was built.   In
his tenth and eleventh years the dedication of a
crown of gold for the god Iau of Kish served as
year-name.   Next year a garden for the gods was
constructed.   So far the reign appears to have been
one of peaceful organisation and consolidation.

In the thirteenth year, however, war broke out,
and Kazallu was raided.   This event seems to have
been commemorated also at Kish under its local
king, but it is ascribed to Sumu-abum.

That Sumu-abum's contest with Assyria terminated favourably is probable, and SUMU-LA-ILU seems to have remained in Assyrian tradition as Sulili, whose kingdom was "very early." It is probable, then, that Sumu-la-ilu was over-lord of Assyria, though it is not named in his reign.

He commenced his reign with the excavation of a canal called the Shamash-khegallu. In his third year a certain Khalambû "was defeated." In his fifth year the great wall of Babylon was built. The seventh, eighth, and ninth years commemorated the building of a temple of Adad. In his tenth year he destroyed Dunnum, and his sway was acknowledged at Lagash. In his twelfth year the canal, Nâr-Sumu-la-ilu, was dug out. The next five years are dated after his capture of Kish. This was undoubtedly a great event, for the older kings of Kish had been over-lords of real empires.

In the eighteenth year Iakhzêr-ilu abandoned Kazallu. Next year the wall of the god Iau, at Kish, was destroyed. Kazallu was now at the mercy of Sumu-la-ilu, and in his twentieth year he destroyed its wall and slew its people. In the twenty-second year a throne adorned with gold and silver was made for the shrine of Marduk. Marduk's consort, Zarpanît, was next presented with her image. Then in the twenty-fifth year Iakhzêr-ilu of Kazallu was slain. Next year the images of Ninni and Nanâ were made. In the twenty-seventh year the wall of Kutha and its temple tower, which had been destroyed, were rebuilt. In his twenty-eighth year Sumu-la-ilu entered Borsippa. The next year he built the wall of Sippara. In the thirtieth year the great temple of Zamama, at Kish, was rebuilt. These were great advances to have made towards the consolidation of the empire.

Unfortunately the date lists furnish no further certain information. Sumu-la-ilu reigned thirty-six years.

Sumu-la-ilu was succeeded by his son, ZABIUM. In the beginning of his reign he built the wall of Kar-Shamash, on the Euphrates. In his eighth year he built the great temple of Ê-babbar for the Sun-god at Sippara. Nabonidus records the finding of his foundation-stone there.

Next year the temple of Ibi-Anum, at Kish, was restored. Then Êsagila was rebuilt. In his eleventh year he made a golden image of himself for the temple of the Sun at Sippara. Kazallu was clearly in his possession, for he rebuilt its wall in his twelfth year. Next year he dug a canal called the Aabba-khégál. His short reign of fourteen years seems to have been without warlike operations, but he was acknowledged king at Lagash in his eleventh year.

Zabium was succeeded by his son, APIL-SIN. In

his first year this king rebuilt the wall of Borsippa.
In his second year he built a new great wall for
Babylon. Next year a throne adorned with gold
and silver was constructed for the shrine of Shamash.
In his fourth year he dug out the canal called Nâr-
Sumudari. In his fifth year Apil-Sin built the wall
of Dûr-mûti. Next year he renewed the great
temple of Nêrgal at Kutha. A throne for Shamash
was next made, perhaps for Sippara. This was
followed by a throne adorned with gold and silver.
A temple to be the dwelling of Ishtar of Babylon
and the temple, Ê-tur-kalamma, were built. In the
sixteenth year the great eastern gate of Babylon
was made, followed next year by a throne for the
shrine of Shamash of Babylon.

Apil-Sin was succeeded by his son, SIN-MUBALLIT,
who in his first year built the wall of Rubatum. It
seems probable that Bêl-dabi, the vassal king of
Assyria, and his wife, possibly a Babylonian princess,
visited Babylon this year. In the next year the
canal, Nâr-Sin-muballit, was dug out. Next year an
altar of incense of gold and precious stones was made
for Shamash. In his fifth year a shrine was made.
The wall for the temple tower was next made. In
the eighth year a canal called the Aia-khégál was
dug. In the tenth year Sin-muballit built the wall
which bore his name. In the eleventh and twelfth
years Karkar and Marad were walled. These

towns lay on the west of the Euphrates, south of
Borsippa. In the thirteenth year the canal called
the Tutu-khégál was dug.

Babylonia had been peacefully developing, and
now Sin-muballit set out on a career of conquest
which laid the foundations of an empire. In the
South, Rîm-Sin had put garrisons in the chief towns
and made Larsa his capital. When, therefore, the
date lists record for the fourteenth year of Sin-
muballit that the army of Ur was crushed, we must
suppose that Rîm-Sin suffered a defeat. It was
followed by the building of the wall of Nanga, and
then by the dedication of a throne for the shrine of
Nergal as king of Kutha. In the seventeenth year
the city of Isin was taken.

In his eighteenth year Sin-muballit built the wall
of Bazu, on the west of the Tigris, not far from
Bagdad. Next year was marked by some dedication
to the gods Shamash and Adad. It seems likely
that the twentieth year was notable for a defeat of
the army of Larsa, but some authorities put this
without question as a variant of the defeat of the
army of Ur in the fourteenth year.

Sin-muballit was succeeded by his son, HAMMURABI,
the most celebrated king of Babylon who ever lived.
He is usually identified with Amraphel, king of Shinar,
named as the ally of Chedorlaomer in Genesis xiv.

In his second year " he established the heart of

*PLATE V*

**Top of Hammurabi's Stele**
*(Code of Laws)*

his land in righteousness," a phrase which has been taken to mean that by his legal reforms he settled the country in law and order. But his great Code of Laws was not promulgated till much later. His reign began peacefully. In his third year he made a throne for the shrine of Nannar of Babylon. Next year he built a wall for Gagia. Then he built two great walls.

In the seventh year the walls of Erech and Isin were taken. In his ninth year Hammurabi dug the canal called after his own name, the Hammurabi-khégál. In his tenth year Malgû, on the Euphrates, was destroyed and its people and cattle carried off. In this year apparently Shamshi-Adad, son of Bêl-dabi, vassal king of Assyria, paid his respects in Babylon. The next year we find that Rabikum and Shalibi were conquered.

In his twelfth year Hammurabi made a throne for Zarpanît, the consort of Marduk. In his four-teenth year a throne for Ishtar of Babylon was made, and then his image in seven exemplars was set up. A throne for Nabû, the image of Ishtar of Kibalbarru, a shrine for Ellil of Babylon, another great wall, a throne for Adad, the wall of Bazu, are events which mark the next six years.

In his twenty-second year a statue of Hammurabi as "king of righteousness" was set up, apparently in the temple of Marduk at Babylon. It was before this statue that the stele containing his great Code was placed.

In his twenty-third year Hammurabi laid the foundation of a wall for Sippara, and after again making a shrine for Ellil, in his twenty-fifth finished the great wall of Sippara. An altar of incense, the temple for Adad, an image of Shala, the consort of Adad, mark the next three years. For the thirtieth year we have the brief note " the year the army of Elam," doubtless indicating their defeat.

In his thirty-first year Hammurabi met with his " crowning mercy." As the fullest form of the date says, " by the help of Anu and Bêl who went before his army his hand smote down the land of Emutbalum and its king, Rîm-Sin." Emutbalum was the homeland of Rîm - Sin, who does not here appear as king of Larsa ; though he probably still held that city, Hammurabi would not acknowledge his title.

Next year the army of Ashnunnak was slain with the sword. This probably means that Hammurabi carried the war into the enemy's land and ravaged the borders of Elam. By his thirty-third year Hammurabi's rule was acknowledged at Nippur.

Then once more the great king turned his attention to works of peace. A canal was dug to bring joy to Ellil. This probably implies that Nippur had opened its gates to him. Then he renewed the temple, Ê-tur-kalamma, for Anu, Ninni and Nanâ, which looks like benefiting Erech. In his thirty-fifth year he rebuilt the ruined walls of Mari and Malgû, on the Euphrates in the North and on the King's Canal in the extreme South. Next he rebuilt the temple of Zamama and Ninni at Kish. In his thirty-seventh year he conquered the people of Turukku, and after a flood which devastated Ashnunnak claims to have reduced by force of arms all the hostile lands of Turukku, Kagmum, and Subartu. In his fortieth year he restored the temple of Nergal at Kutha, and next year built a great wall on the bank of the Tigris and raised its head mountain-high, and called its name Kar-Shamash. The same year the wall of Rabikum, on the Euphrates, was rebuilt. A canal called Tishid-Ellil was dug for the benefit of Sippara, but at present its date is uncertain. In the forty-third year a great mound was built along the moat of Sippara, to the honour of Shamash.

In the prologue to the Code, Hammurabi recalls the benefits he conferred on his land, naming Nippur and Dûrilu, on the borders of Elam; Eridu, Ur, Sippara, Larsa, Erech, Isin, Kish, Kutha, Borsippa, Dilbat, Lagash, Aleppo (?), Karkar, Mashganshabri, Malgû, Mera and Tultul, Agade, Asshur, Nineveh, besides the settlements on the Euphrates.

A few of his inscriptions have been preserved

which add little to our knowledge. They record his buildings at temples, etc., the digging of the Nukhush-nishi canal, at the head of which he built a fortress called Dûr-Sin-muballit, to perpetuate his father's name.

SAMSU-ILUNA succeeded his father, Hammurabi, and apparently had to face difficulties at once. In his first year he made claim to rule over foreign lands by force. In the next year " he established the freedom of Sumer and Akkad." In his third year he dug a canal called after him, and next year another. Then he made a golden throne for the shrine of Nannar. In his sixth year he made pedestals in Ê-babbar before Shamash, and in Êsagila before Marduk, and placed upon them golden statues representing himself in an attitude of prayer. In his seventh year he dedicated to Marduk in Êsagila a censer and a gold and silver mace. Next year he made a brazen stand, representing mountains and rivers carrying abundance to the lands.

In his ninth year there occurred an incursion of the Kassites. We may gather that they were defeated, but next year Samsu-iluna had to fight the Idamaraz, an otherwise unknown people. Doubtless they also were crushed, but it was clearly a struggle in which Rîm-Sin took a hand, for we find that Emutbalum was also defeated, Isin and

Erech probably captured. How long these two
cities had been alienated is not easy to see, but
certainly Rîm-Sin was acknowledged king in Larsa
in this year. Chronicle K 1 records the fall of Rîm-
Sin's capital and his capture in his palace. Samsu-
iluna went on, in his eleventh year, to rebuild the
walls of Ur and Erech, which had been destroyed.
Finally Samsu-iluna subdued all the lands which
had revolted from him. Next he chastised and
subdued Kisurra and Sabum. In his fourteenth
year he appears as having subdued a pretender
whom the Akkadians had set up. In his fifteenth
year he rebuilt the wall of Isin, which had been
destroyed. Next year he restored the wall of
Sippara. In his seventeenth year he restored the
destroyed fortresses in Emutbalum, which he had
evidently now added to his dominions.

It was a great achievement to have thus won
back his father's empire. Henceforward Samsu-
iluna repaired damages. In his eighteenth year he
renewed Êbabbar, the temple of Shamash in Sippara ;
next year dedicated two golden thrones for Marduk ;
made some further dedication next year ; made a
throne for Ningal in the great golden chamber
which sparkled like the stars of heaven ; next year
renovated the temple tower for Zamama's temple
at Kish, thus renewing the chief places of worship
in the land.

F

In his twenty-third year Samsu-iluna destroyed
the wall of Shakhnâ and the city of Zarkhanum.
Next year he built a wall for Kish, called " the
wall whose glory fills the lands," on the Euphrates
canal, and a wall called after himself on the Arakhtu
canal. Then his own image was erected representing him as smiting down his enemies with his
mace. In his twenty-sixth year the marvel selected
to be commemorated was his transport of a huge
monolith of basalt from the land of Amurrû, perhaps the Amanus range. The chief wonder was
its size, twenty-two cubits long. Next year a
great dedication for the New Year Festival took
place.

Then arose a severe struggle. Two foes whose
names, Iadikhabu and Mûti-khurshana, suggest
that they were of the Amorite stock, were finally
crushed. In his thirty-first year Samsu-iluna set
up an image of himself grasping a mace of glitter-
ing gold. Next year the canal at Sippara, in the
thirty-third year the restoration of the city Sag-
garatum, then a princely door for the temple
occupied his attention. Events not over clear at
Amal and Arkum, the army of Amurrû, a trouble
in Akkad, and finally, in his thirty-eighth year, the
dedication of a weapon for Ninib, the warrior god,
are recorded as marking the years of this highly
successful king.

In his building inscriptions he records the restoration of six fortresses which had been founded
by Sumu-la-ilu, " his fifth forefather." In absorbing the domains of Rîm-Sin he became neighbour
to Ilu-ma-ilu, king of the Sealand, first king of the
Uru-azagga dynasty. The details of the resulting
conflict are very obscure, but Chronicle K 1 records
a siege and a battle in which dead bodies were
washed away by the sea. Again Samsu-iluna
attacked Ilu-ma-ilu, but was beaten off, and left
the struggle to his son.

ABÊSHU' succeeded his father. By a strange
fatality all the date lists are so defective that we
cannot arrange the events of his reign in chronological order. We know from dated documents
many of these events, which were largely of a
pious nature, such as adorning or restoring temples,
digging canals, etc.

The Sealand was now fast rising into power, and
Ilu-ma-ilu was able to found a dynasty there.
Abêshu' ineffectually attempted to thwart his
ambition. The southern people lived amid inaccessible swamps, and Abêshu' dammed up the
Tigris canal in order to penetrate the district, but
though he was able to defeat Ilu-ma-ilu, that
king escaped capture.

Abêshu' built a city, Lukhaia, on the Arakhtu canal,
but on the whole we are unable to record any very

noteworthy achievement.   He reigned twenty-eight years.

An obscure record points to a fresh invasion by the Kassites.   One of the images Abêshu' set up was that of the deified Entemena.   Abêshu' was succeeded by his son, AMMIDITANA.   The first fifteen years of his reign were marked by peaceful and pious works, temple adornments, images of himself in attitudes of worship, thrones for the shrines, while the wall of Kar-Shamash on the Euphrates, a wall named after himself along the Zilakum canal, are commemorated.   Then in his seventeenth year he put down a Sumerian rising under Arakhab.   The great cloister, Gagia, was next restored.   Again the works of piety and utility went on.   The wall, Ishkun-Marduk, on the Zilakum canal, may be noted.   In his thirty-fourth year an image of Samsu-iluna, his ancestor " the warrior king," was set up in Kish, actually a century after his accession.   A wall called after himself along the canal Mê-Ellil was built at Kish.

The name of his last year has given rise to much speculation.   It records that he destroyed a wall at *Bad-ki* which the men of Damki-ilishu had built. It has been thought that by *Bad-ki*, the city of Isin is intended.   Damki-ilishu was the name of the third king of the dynasty of the Sealand and also of the last king of Isin.   This latter was, as we

know, a contemporary of Hammurabi, and cannot
be intended here, unless the reference be to a wall
formerly set up by that king.

AMMIZADUGA succeeded his father, Ammiditana.
The date lists give the events of his first sixteen
years in chronological order, and he appears to
have reigned twenty-two years in all. None of
the year-names so far known record any warlike
operations. Temple adornments, images of himself as worshipping his gods, a wall on the Euphrates, the inevitable canal, mark a reign peaceful,
pious, and prosperous.

Ammizaduga was succeeded by his son, SAMSU-
DITANA. The existing date lists give us no information as to his reign, but the Babylonian List
of Kings A gives him a reign of thirty-one years,
and about thirty year-names are known. They are
mostly of the pious order, dedications of images of
himself or of the gods, or the construction of thrones
for shrines.

Chronicle K 1 states " that in his days the men
of the land of Khatti marched against the land of
Akkad." It does not say how the battle went, nor
in which year of his reign it fell.

It may well be that this HITTITE INVASION made
an end of the First Dynasty of Babylon. We know
that the capital of the Hittite kingdom was at
Boghaz-köi, whose old name was Khatti, and that

about this time the Hittites became lords of Mesopotamia, conquering the kings of Mitanni, who
just previously had conquered Assyria. It may
well be that the Kassites were a branch of these
Hittites. The Kassites are usually supposed to
have descended into Babylonia, and either conquered the land or gradually risen to power there,
from the mountain districts where later the
Assyrian conquerors found them in power. But
this district itself may have been conquered by
them at this time, and only formed their retreat in
later years after their expulsion from Babylonia.

In any case, we may well suppose that the
Hittite invasion so weakened Babylonia that it
fell a prey to the Kassites after no very long
interval. Marduk was twenty-four years in the
Hittite land, as we are told by a later hymn.

THE SECOND DYNASTY.—As the Kings' List
placed a dynasty of kings, called that of Uru-
azagga, next after the First Dynasty of Babylon,
it has been usual to suppose that they immediately
succeeded. But of late years it has become evident that they really formed a dynasty of kings
who primarily ruled the Sealand, and it is doubtful
whether they ever ruled over North Babylonia
at all.

The list is : Ilu-ma-ilu, 60 years ; Kiannibi, 56
years ; Damki-ilishu II., 26 years ; Ishkibal, 15

years ; Shushshi, 24 years ; Gulkishar, 55 years ; Kirgal-daramash, 50 years ; Adara-kalama, 28 years ; Akur-ulanna, 26 years ; Melam-kurkurra, 8 years ; and Ea-gamil, 20 years. There are eleven kings with a total duration of 368 years.

The average length of reign is unusual, and would suggest only peaceful development and prosperity. The synchronisms between Assyrian rulers and the First Dynasty, compared with those between later rulers and the Kassite kings, make it very difficult to accept the view that 368 years lay between the reigns of Samsu-ditana and the first Kassite king. But the various attempts made to reconcile the data leave such uncertainty that we can only say the evidence is not sufficient to prove either that this dynasty ruled in Babylonia, or that, if so, its length of supremacy can be ascertained.

There is a remarkable absence of monuments of these kings, but a few notices of them have come down to us which negative the conclusions drawn by some historians that they were either fictitious or insignificant.

Thus we know from the later Babylonian Chronicles that Ilu-ma-ilu warred with Samsu-iluna and Abêshu'. We have no hint as to the fortunes of either state during the last three reigns of the First Dynasty, some ninety years, which would cover at least the first three years of the Sealand kings. We shall note their end later. Ammikinabi may be the real name of the second king, as it appears on a dated document about this period.

# CHAPTER VII

## THE KASSITE OR THIRD DYNASTY

THE Kassites are frequently named in the Babylonian contract tablets chiefly as workpeople, harvesters, or builders, from the tenth year of Hammurabi onwards, at Sippara, Dilbat, and Kish. They are registered as in receipt of corn and drink, probably as rations during their working period, and enter into leases of fields on the same terms as the native Babylonians down to the reign of Samsu-ditana. Presumably the Kassites were defeated in the ninth year of Samsu-iluna.

It is usually considered that the horse was introduced to the Babylonians by the Kassites, because so few references to horses have been found in the period of the First Dynasty.

The names borne by the Kassite kings and their people, who formed a not very numerous aristocracy in Babylonia, although they also appear in humbler walks of life, are thought to have marked affinities with those of Elamites. There exists a small collection of Kassite words, probably compiled with a view to interpreting proper names, and a few titles and terms occur scattered through

the business documents of the period. From these
scanty remains of their language it is impossible
definitely to classify them racially or linguistically.
They have been identified with the Kossæans and
the Kissians of Greek writers. They are usually
called Kassites by modern scholars, with some
justification, as the Babylonians always named
them Kashshû, or in the plural, Kashshî. Sennacherib gave this name to the people whom he conquered in the hills above Holwan, about the sources
of the Diyala. Earlier Assyrian monarchs record
their conquests of the Kashshû, to the east of
their own land, in the mountains.

Very few inscriptions are as yet recovered which
are of much direct service for history. The Synchronous History, as far as it concerns this period,
gives our chief information as to their relations
with Assyria. The Kings' List A gave a full list of
the names of thirty-six kings, of which only the
first six names and the last eleven are preserved.
It states the total duration of the dynasty to have
been 576 years and nine months. The numerous
tablets discovered at Nippur belonging to the end
of this period have added several names to the list,
and the patient piecing together of small items of
information by various scholars has restored many
more. The most extensive discoveries of late
have been at Susa under De Morgan, chiefly

of monuments carried thither by the Elamite conquerors.

The Kassites gave the name of Karduniash to the territory over which they ruled in the South of Babylonia, as against Babylon and Akkad, and they early included the Sealand in it. The Assyrians regarded it as the name of the whole of Babylonia ; but by the time of Sennacherib it seems to have been confined to the Sealand.

GANDASH, or Gaddash, the king placed first on the Kings' List A, reigned sixteen years. A late copy, made in 287 B.C., of an inscription of his shows that he claimed to be king of the four quarters, king of Sumer and Akkad, king of Babylon. He rebuilt the temple of Ellil, which had been destroyed in the capture of Babylon. He calls Nippur his city. AGUM I. reigned twenty-two years, as did KASHTILIASH I., but we do not know the lengths of reign of the next three kings, USHSHI, ABIRATTASH, and TASHSHIGURUMASH.

AGUM II., or AGUM KAKRIME, probably came next. An inscription of his, extending to 134 lines in eight columns, is in Semitic Babylonian, and begins with a genealogy. He names his father, Tashshigurumash ; his grandfather, Abirattash, son of Kashtiliash, the eldest (?) son of Agum the great, who, further, was son of Gandash. The omission of Ushshi is best explained by supposing him to be

brother of Kashtiliash I. The Kings' List is thus
confirmed fully. Agum II. styles himself king of
the Kassites and Akkadians, king of Babylon, who
settled with people the land of Ashnunnak, king
of Padan and Alman, king of Gutium and the
Saklâti folk. He goes on to relate that Marduk
and his consort, Zarpanît, had been carried away
to the far-off land of Khani (Mitanni), and Agum,
after consulting Shamash the Sun-god by means
of augury, sent and brought them back to Babylon,
and restored them to Êsagila, which he renovated
and furnished for their reception with great
splendour. Gold and all manner of precious stones
and rare woods were lavished upon the adornment
of the images and their shrines. The dragon, the
goat, the fish-men, goat-fish, and other monsters,
over whom Marduk was fabled to have triumphed
at the Creation, were carved in precious stones.
He restored the priesthood and the cult, and endowed it with house, field and garden free from
tax. He has become a thorough Babylonian, the
only touch of Kassite influence is that in the very
first sentence he calls himself " illustrious seed of
Shuqamuna," the Kassite war-god.

BURNABURIASH I. has been placed next, because
a late Babylonian Chronicle records that Eagamil's
expedition to Elam was followed by an invasion of
the Sealand by Ulamburiash, brother of Kashtiliash

the Kassite. Further, a mace-head was found at Babylon belonging to Ulamburiash, son of Burnaburiash, the king who calls himself king of the Sealand. We can scarcely doubt that he was also king of Babylon, and that his son succeeded him as KASHTILIASH II.

AGUM III.—According to the same late Babylonian Chronicle, one Agum, son of a Kashtiliash, invaded the Sealand, captured Dûr-Êa and destroyed its temple. He would thus be the nephew of Ulamburiash, whose conquest of the Sealand he was called upon to repeat.

A king, NAZI-ELLIL, is referred to as the ancestor of one of the kings in the Nippur series, in a letter addressed to that king. We may provisionally place him at the head of the list.

The earliest of the kings whose names and order we can fix is KARA-INDASH I. He made a treaty with Ashur-bêl-nishêshu, king of Assyria, about their boundary. He seems to have corresponded with Thothmes III., king of Egypt. A short inscription of his calls him king of Babylon, Sumer and Akkad, as well as of Karduniash and the Kassites. He rebuilt the temple Ê-anna at Erech.

It must remain doubtful whether KURIGALZU I., whose descendant Burnaburiash II. represents him as in friendly correspondence with the Egyptian kings, came before or after Kara-indash I. It is

not unlikely that to him we must ascribe the foundation of Dûr-Kurigalzu as a fortress to guard his
northern frontier. It soon became an important
city. His grandson, Marduk-aplu-iddin I., speaks
of him as " unrivalled king."

From the correspondence of the Kassite kings
with those of Egypt, we learn that one KADASHMAN-
ELLIL was contemporary with Amenophis III.,
and addressed three letters to him, while Amenophis
kept copies of two letters which he had addressed
to Kadashman-Ellil.

Chronicle P relates that KADASHMAN-KHARBE,
son of Kara-khardash, (and) son of Muballitat-
sherûa, daughter of Ashur-uballit, king of Assyria,
carried out the subjugation of the predatory Sutû
from east to west. He also erected fortresses in
Amurrû and dug wells. To secure their protection
he settled a large population round them. Later,
the Kassites rebelled against him, killed him, and
raised SHUZIGASH, a Kassite of humble origin, to
be king over them. Whereupon Ashur-uballit,
king of Assyria, marched into Karduniash to
avenge Kadashman-Kharbe, his daughter's son,
slew Shuzigash the Kassite, and set Kurigalzu, " a
child," son of Kadashman-Kharbe, on the throne
of his father.

The Synchronous History, after its entry about
Kara-indash I., states that Buzur-Ashur, king of

Assyria, and Burnaburiash, king of Karduniash, made a fresh boundary treaty confirming the previous agreement. This statement may also have stood in Chronicle P, but the traces before the above account of Kadashman-Kharbe seem to refer to a king of Karduniash who made a boundary treaty with a king of Assyria, who is not Buzur-Ashur, but could be either Ashur-bêl-nishêshu or Ashur-uballit. They appear to have returned something (an image of a god ?) to its place in Kharsagkalamma. One expects that here were given the relations of Kara-khardash with Ashur-uballit.

Now the Tell-el-Amarna tablets show that a Burnaburiash, king of Karduniash, corresponded possibly with Amenophis III., certainly wrote five letters to Amenophis IV., and also exchanged presents with that king. This Burnaburiash, therefore, came to the throne soon after Kadash-man-Ellil. He mentions as his "father" or "fore-father," one Kurigalzu, who was in friendly relations with the "father" of Amenophis IV. We have denoted him as Kurigalzu I. above.

Further, Ashur-uballit, king of Assyria, wrote at least one letter to Amenophis IV.

The Synchronous History inserts after Burna-buriash a paragraph which has given rise to most complicated discussions. It states that "in the time

of Ashur-uballit, king of Assyria, Kara-khardash king
of Karduniash the son of Muballitat-sherûa daughter
of Ashur-uballit the Kassites rebelled and slew him."
Here it seems to be obvious that the scribe has
omitted some lines. Then the scribe goes on cor-
rectly thus :—" They raised to the kingship over
them Nazibugash the son of a nobody. Ashur-
uballit went to Karduniash to avenge Kara-indash."
Beside the misreading, Nazibugash for Shuzigash, the
scribe must have written Kara-indash for Kara-
khardash owing to his mistake of the latter for
Kadashman-Kharbe. Then he states that Ashur-
uballit established Kurigalzu, " the child," son of
Burnaburiash, on the throne of his father.

The next entry in the Synchronous History records
that Kurigalzu, " the child," king of Karduniash,
and Bêl-nirari, king of Assyria, waged war and
fought at Sugagi. Bêl-nirari captured his camp
and baggage. They then divided between them
the fields from Shubari to Karduniash, and made
a treaty. Chronicle P seems to have a very
similar entry at the end of a reign of one Kurigalzu,
but after a successful campaign against Elam, where
we read that " Against Adad-nirari king of Assyria
to the land . . . in Sugaga, on the river Tsaltsallat . . . he slew his soldiers his nobles. . . ."
Now we know that KURIGALZU III. made a successful raid into Elam, but he was son of Burnaburiash

and was succeeded by Nazimarattash, who comes
in the next section on P. This fight at Sugagi
took place then in the time of Kurigalzu III. It
is separated by a whole column from the events
by which Kurigalzu II. came to the throne. Adad-
nirari was grandson of Bêl-nirari.

In a legal decision of this period the plaintiff
claims to have held certain lands from the time of
Kurigalzu (II.), son of Kadashman-Kharbe, until
that of Nazimarattash, son of Kurigalzu (III.).
If these had been one and the same Kurigalzu, the
space of time would have been expressed as from
the time of Kurigalzu to that of his son, a quite
pointless mode of expression. An inscription of
Kurigalzu, son of Kadashman-Kharbe, set up by
one Ellil-bani, priest of Ellil, calls him " the unrivalled king."

BURNABURIASH III. reigned at least twenty-five
years. In his inscriptions he calls himself king of
Babylon, of Sumer and Akkad.

KURIGALZU III., son of Burnaburiash III., reigned
at least twenty-three years. He has left many
votive offerings found at Nippur. He captured
from the palace of Susa in Elam an agate tablet
which had once been dedicated by a *patesi* in Babylonia for the life of Dungi, king of Ur, to the goddess
Ninni. Kurigalzu now brought it back and dedicated it to Nin-lil of Nippur, " his mistress," for

G

his own life. Khurbatila, king of Elam, sent a challenge to Kurigalzu, saying, " Come, I and thou will fight together." Kurigalzu accepted the challenge, set out to Elam and met Khurbatila, whose troops deserted. Kurigalzu defeated and captured the king of Elam with his own hand. " So Kurigalzu received tribute from the kings of all lands." Later he attacked Adad-nirari, king of Assyria, and fought him at Sugaga, on the river Tsaltsallat, slew his soldiers and captured his nobles.

NAZIMARATTASH, son of Kurigalzu III., reigned twenty-four years. He fought with Adad-nirari I. in Kar-Ishtar and Akarsallu. Adad-nirari I. defeated him with great slaughter and captured his camp and standards. Then they made a boundary treaty and divided the lands from Pilasqi, on the Tigris, to the Lullume. He has left several inscriptions at Nippur.

KADASHMAN-TURGU reigned seventeen years : he was son of Nazimarattash, and left several inscriptions at Nippur.

KADASHMAN-ELLIL II. reigned twelve years according to the Kings' List. He was son of Kadashman-turgu.

KUDUR-ELLIL reigned eight years at least. He was son of Kadashman-Ellil II.

SHAGARAKTI-SHURIASH reigned thirteen years

According to Nabonidus he was son of Kudur-
Ellil, and built Ê-ulmash 800 years before the time
of Nabonidus. He repaired the temple of the
Sun-god in Sippara.

KASHTILIASH III. reigned eight years. He was
son of Shagarakti-shuriash. Tukulti-Ninip I.
defeated Kashtiliash, took him prisoner to Assyria,
and led him in chains before Ashur, the national
god. He then destroyed the city wall of Babylon
and massacred its defenders. He carried away
the treasures of Êsagila and Babylon and the great
god Marduk himself to Assyria. Among the
treasures was a seal of Shagarakti-shuriash, who
claimed the title *shar kishshati* upon it, this
Tukulti-Ninip had engraved with his own titles,
as *shar kishshati*, and deposited it in his temple.
Somewhat later it was stolen from Assyria and
given back to Akkad, where Sennacherib found it
among the treasures of Babylon, and records that
he had brought it back again after 600 years.

According to Chronicle P, Tukulti-Ninip I. set
viceroys over Karduniash, and ruled it for seven
years, the Kings' List A does not, however,
include him among the rulers of Babylonia. After
his death in an insurrection he was succeeded for
a short time by his son, Ashur-natsir-pal I. Then
came a period of great disturbance in Assyria, and
evidently its hold on Babylonia was relaxed.

The Kings' List A gives as the next king of Babylonia one ELLIL-NÂDIN-SHUM, with a reign of one year and six months. Chronicle P relates of him that he went out and attacked Kidin-Khutrudash, king of Elam, who had laid his hands on Nippur and massacred its people. He captured Dûr-ili and Kharsagkalama, and drove out the Elamites from them.

The Kings' List A gives KADASHMAN-KHARBE II. as the next king, with a reign of one year and six months.

Then the Kings' List gives ADAD-SHUM-IDDINA a reign of six years. When Kidin-Khutrudash invaded Babylonia a second time, Adad-shum-iddina seems to have fought him at Isin. The Tigris entirely flooded the district. This king overthrew many people.

The end of this reign would account for the sixteen years during which Chronicle P says that the statue of Marduk remained in Assyria. It went back to Babylon in the time of Tukulti-Ashur. The next king in Babylonia was ADAD-SHUM-UTSUR, who reigned thirty years. Two letters were sent to Assyrian kings by Adad-shum-utsur. One is addressed to two kings, Ashur-nirari and Nabû-dân, who seem to be reigning together, and refers to unrest in Assyria and to a certain Adad-shum-lishir. The other names neither Adad-shum-utsur,

*PLATE VI*

Kudurru of Melishipak

nor the king of Assyria to whom it was addressed. But the king of Babylonia who writes it repels an offer of friendship. He does not acknowledge the *fait accompli*. He points out that a king of Assyria, Ninib-tukulti-Ashur, obviously the Tukulti-Ashur of Chronicle P, had fled to him to Babylon, leaving his representative, Ashur-shum-lishir, in power. The rebels in Assyria rose against Ninib-tukulti-Ashur in his absence, expelled his *locum tenens*, and now demanded his surrender, which Adad-shum-utsur refused. Whether he had fled, or merely gone on a friendly mission to Babylonia, does not appear ; but he probably took with him the statue of Marduk and possibly the seal of Shagarakti-shuriash, carried off with it by Tukulti-Ninip I.

The Synchronous History relates a war between Adad-shum-utsur and Ellil-kudur-utsur, king of Assyria. Apparently the latter was killed in battle. His son or general retired to Asshur, whither Adad-shum-utsur pursued him, and besieged Asshur but was unable to capture it.

The next king, MELI-SHIPAK, to whom the Kings' List A gives a reign of fifteen years, bore a Kassite name although son of Adad-shum-utsur. He was king of Babylon and *shar kishshati*.

MARDUK - APLU - IDDIN I., son of Meli-shipak, reigned thirteen years. He, too, was king of Babylon and *shar kishshati*, and calls himself descendant of Kurigalzu I., "the unrivalled king," king of Sumer and Akkad.

ZAMAMA-SHUM-IDDIN, to whom the Kings' List assigns but one year, had to stand an invasion by Ashur-dân, king of Assyria, who captured the cities Zaban, Irria, and Akarsallu, carrying off a heavy booty to Assyria.  An Elamite king, father of one Kudurnankhundi, deposed him.  This king must be Shutruk-nankhundi.  The Elamites at this time made a terrific spoliation of Babylonia.  Repeatedly we have noted "found at Susa" of some Babylonian monument.  In such cases, we may take for granted that this was the occasion on which it was carried off.

BÊL-SHUM-IDDIN next reigned for three years.

Thus the Kassite Dynasty ended after a duration of 576 years and nine months, according to the Kings' List A.

Some scholars, relying upon an inscription naming one Meli-shipak, son of Marduk-aplu-iddina, give a Meli-shipak II. and Marduk-aplu-iddin II. as kings of this dynasty; but their place, and even their existence, are uncertain.  To avoid confusion the Merodach baladan of the bible is here called "the third."

# CHAPTER VIII

## The Fourth Dynasty

THE Kings' List A calls this the dynasty of Isin (II.).
It may be that its early rulers were contemporary
with the last kings of the Third Dynasty. For,
when Shutruk-nankhundi had deposed Zamama-
shum-iddin, he probably set his son, Kudur-nankhundi, upon the throne of Babylon. The Kings'
List, however, credited Bêl-shum-iddin with a
reign of two or three years. This can hardly be
the same as ELLIL-NÂDIN-AKHI, who, as Nebuchadrezzar I. states, threw off the yoke of Elam. The
Kings' List may be supposed to have ignored the
Elamite usurpers, but gave the first king of this
dynasty a name beginning with Marduk, and ascribed
to him a reign of eighteen years. Possibly this unknown king reigned at Isin only.

ELLIL-NÂDIN-AKHI may thus be the second king
of the dynasty who reigned six years.

NEBUCHADREZZAR I. succeeded. He was defeated
at Dûr-Apil-Sin, but finally triumphed. He carried
the war into the enemy's country and subdued the
Kassites and the Lullume. He conquered the
Amorite land.

From a *kudurru* inscription we learn that the Elamites had annexed the district of Namar, famous for its horse-breeding. Assisted by the local chief, Ritti-Marduk, Nebuchadrezzar attacked the Elamites who held Dûr-ilu. He drove them out, and pursuing them across the Tigris, brought them to bay on the banks of the river Ulai, where he utterly routed them, and then raided Elam, capturing great spoil. In the battles, Ritti-Marduk had ridden at the king's right hand, and on his return, Nebuchadrezzar reinvested him with his ancestral possession, restored its special privileges, exempted it from taxes and dues. We may note that troops from Nippur and Babylon were stationed in Namar as its garrison, and the monument bears the attestation of high officials of Babylon, Halman, Akkad, and Isin.

Shamua and Shamai, sons of the priest Nûr-lishir, as we learn from another *kudurru*, escaped to Karduniash from Elam whither they had been carried prisoners. Nebuchadrezzar returned with them, plundered Elam, and took the hands of the captive Marduk and the goddess Eria. Marduk he brought back to Babylon, and restored Eria to Khutstsi. He then endowed the two priests with lands in Opis and Dûr-Sargon.

When Nebuchadrezzar attacked the Assyrian fortress of Zanqi, Ashur-rêsh-ishi, king of Assyria, compelled him to abandon the siege. When he later sent an army against Assyria he was again defeated, lost his general, Karashtu, and forty war chariots. The men of Khatti invaded Babylonia in his third year and took Babylon, but Nebuchadrezzar collected his troops, and in thirteen days (from Isin ?) drove them out, conquered Ammananu, and cut off the heads of the inhabitants. This may have been the occasion of his invasion of the West Land when he seems to have reached the Mediterranean.

He was not only a warrior. He brought tablets of the great work on augury, usually known as the Illumination of Bêl, from Babylon (to Isin ?), imported scribes and made a tablet depicting "The Lady of Heaven " with her decrees and the Motions of the Stars. He was the son of Ninib-nâdin-shum, who, however, is not called a king. His reign lasted at least sixteen years.

ELLIL-NÂDIN-APLI succeeded Nebuchadrezzar I., and reigned at least four years.

MARDUK-NÂDIN-AKHE succeeded Ellil-nâdin-apli, and reigned at least ten years. He bore the title *shar kishshati* as well as king of Babylon. On a *kudurru* he granted an estate to Adad-zêr-iqisha, his servant, who had served him well in the conflict with Assyria. The Synchronous History records that he and Tiglath-pileser I. set their chariots in array " for the second time " near Arzukhina. In

the second year they fought in Marriti above the
land of Akkad, and the Assyrian captured Dûr-
Kurigalzu, Sippar of Shamash, Sippar Anunitum,
Babylon and Opis. Then the Assyrian plundered
Akar-sallu down to Lubdi and subdued the land of
Sukhi as far as Rapiki. Marduk-nâdin-akhe had
evidently fought with Tiglath-pileser a "first"
time, and he probably then defeated the Assyrians.
He captured Adad and Shala, the gods of Ekallate,
and carried them to Babylonia, whence they were
brought back by Sennacherib.

MARDUK-SHÂPIK-ZÊRIM    probably    succeeded
Marduk-nâdin-akhe, as he entered into friendly
relations with Ashur-bêl-kala, who was son of
Tiglath-pileser I. From Assyria, where he seems
to have gone on a friendly visit, he went to Sippar,
which may have been restored to him to cement
the treaty.

He rebuilt and enlarged Ê-zida, rebuilt the walls
of Babylon, and ruled over a prosperous and extensive empire. Towards the end of his reign, his
subjects in Karduniash rebelled and placed Adad-
aplu-iddina as king over them.

ADAD-APLU-IDDINA succeeded. The Synchronous History calls him son of Êsagil-shadûni, son of
a nobody, and Chronicle K makes him son of Itti-
Marduk-balâtu. The Aramæans plundered the cities
of Akkad up to Paddiri and Dûr-ilu. The Sutû

raided Babylonia and carried off the plunder of Sumer and Akkad. This king restored the temples of Marduk and other gods. He rebuilt Nimit-Marduk, the outer wall of Nippur. He reigned at least ten years. Ashur-bêl-kala, king of Assyria, married his daughter and took her with her rich dowry to Assyria, and the peoples of the two countries were united in friendship. It should be noted that ITTI-MARDUK-BALÂTU was certainly a king, who may well have been the real father of this monarch, and a usurper. If so, he may have directly succeeded Marduk-shâpik-zêrim. He calls himself son of Marduk-kabti-akhi, and takes the same titles as Kurigalzu and Hammurabi.

MARDUK-AKHÊ-ERBA is placed next by some scholars, though others would place him at the head of the dynasty.

The Kings' List A retains the beginning of three more royal names. Marduk-bêl . . . reigned one year and a half; Marduk-zêr . . . reigned thirteen years; and NABÛ-SHUM-LIBUR reigned nine years. His name occurs on a duck-shaped weight of thirty minas, in the British Museum, which gives him the title *shar kishshati*.

THE FIFTH DYNASTY.—The Kings' List A assigns to this dynasty, which it calls that of " The Sealand," three kings, with a total duration of twenty years and three months.

The first king was Simbar-shîpak, who reigned
eighteen years. He was a *corvée* master, son of
Erba-Sin. After a reign of seventeen years he
was slain with the sword, and buried in the palace
of Sargon. Nabû-aplu-iddin states that he restored the great temple of Shamash in Sippara.
The Sutû had destroyed it, and Simbar-shîpak
sought for the ancient representation of Shamash,
but was unable to find it. However, he surrounded
the old temple with a wall and restored its revenues.
He was succeeded by ÊA-MUKÎN-ZÊR, who is called
a usurper by the Dynastic Chronicle, and stated to
have been " son " of Khashmar. He was buried
in the swamps of Bît-Khashmar, after a reign of
only a few months.

KASHSHU-NÂDIN-AKHI is given a reign of three
years by the Kings' List A. The Dynastic Chronicle
calls him son of Sippâ. He was buried in the
palace of Sargon. Nabû-aplu-iddin says that in
the want and disturbances of this reign, the offerings and observances of the temple of Shamash
again fell into desuetude.

THE SIXTH DYNASTY.—According to the Kings'
List A, this dynasty of Bazu consisted of three
kings, with a total duration of twenty years and
six months.

Ê-ULMASH-SHÂKIN-SHUM reigned seventeen years.
He was buried in the palace of Etir-Marduk. Nabû-

aplu-iddin says that Êkur-shum-ubshabshi, the priest of Shamash at Sippara, petitioned this king for a grant and was allowed rations from the superintendent of Êsagila. This king further granted him an estate in the New-city.

From a table of portents it appears that a great storm occurred in the seventh year, and, in the eleventh year, such a deluge that the waters came within the wall of the Lower Mound (in Babylon ?).

NINIP-KUDURRI-UTSUR reigned three years.

SHILANUM-SHUQAMUNA reigned three months.

THE SEVENTH DYNASTY.—AE-APLU-UTSUR, the Elamite, reigned six years, and was buried in the palace of Sargon.

THE EIGHTH DYNASTY.—The Kings' List A begins with a reign of perhaps thirty-six years, followed by one of eight months and perhaps twelve days, but gives no names. Later, it preserves four names, and gives a total duration of perhaps fifty-two years to the Dynasty of E-ki.

NABÛ-MUKIN-APLI is generally taken to be the first king of the Dynasty, as a *kudurru*, dated in his twenty-fourth year, seems to reckon from the second year of Ninib-kudurri-utsur to the fifth year of this king as seven (?) years. This would exclude the reign of the Elamite. Hence some would place a Ninib-kudurri-utsur as third, and Nabû-mukin-apli as fourth in this dynasty.

A number of portents have been recorded for the various years of this reign. In Nisan of his seventh year the Aramæans were at war, and the king could not go up to Babylon, nor was it possible for Nabû to go thither from Borsippa. Next year, at the same time, the Aramæans having captured the Ferry Gate of Kar-bêl-mâtâti, the king could not cross over and so could not go to Babylon. So Nabû stayed in Borsippa, and Bêl did not go out. The same thing occurred in the nineteenth, twentieth, and nine succeeding years. A great storm occurred in the twenty-sixth year. He reigned at least twenty-eight years.

After one or two kings, at present unknown, we have traces ending in . . . akhî-iddina, which may be part of the name of a Babylonian king, not yet identified.

SHAMASH-MUDAMMIQ is next named by Chronicle K, in conjunction with Adad-nirari III., king of Assyria. From the Synchronous History we learn that he set his battle array at the foot of Mount Ialman, and there Adad-nirari defeated him and captured his horses and chariots. Then Nabû-shum-ishkun I. killed Shamash-mudammiq and came to the throne.

NABÛ-SHUM-ISHKUN I. had to fight for his crown with Adad-nirari III., who carried the war into Babylonia, defeated Nabû-shum-ishkun, captured

*PLATE VII*

**Tablet of Nabû-aplu-iddin**

*(With terra-cotta coverings for protecting the sculpture)*

the cities of Baribala and Khudadu, and carried off a great spoil to Assyria. The Babylonian monarch retired to the fastnesses of his land. Later he exchanged matrimonial alliances with Adad-nirari and made peace with him. The Synchronous History adds that Assyria and Karduniash then lived in amity, and settled their boundary from Tilbari, on the Zaban, to Til-sha-batani and Til-sha-zabdani.

Nabû-shum-ishkûn was also contemporary with Tukulti-Ninip II., king of Assyria.

NABÛ-APLU-IDDIN was son of Nabû-shum-ukîn. He has left a stone tablet recording his restoration of the temple and cult of Shamash at Sippara. His notices of earlier kings we have quoted above. He confirmed, restored, and augmented the endowments conferred by earlier kings, made a statue of rich gold and bright lapis-lazuli to represent his god, and set it up in a magnificent shrine; ordered the daily offerings, endowed special festivals with rich robes for the god, and installed Nabû-nâdin-shum as priest. The deed was dated in his thirty-first year. The Synchronous History relates that he made close alliance with Shalmaneser II., king of Assyria. In 879 B.C. he actively supported the Sukhi on the south bank of the Euphrates against Ashur-natsirpal IV., king of Assyria, sending his own brother, Zabdanu, to resist him. The Assyrian, however, gained the victory and captured Zab-danu with 3000 of his troops.

Nabû-aplu-iddin appears to have left the throne of Babylonia to his son, MARDUK-ZÂKIR-SHUM, whose brother, Marduk-bêl-usâte, king of the eastern provinces, contested his title and pressed him hard. Marduk-zâkir-shum appealed to Shalmaneser III. and was at once supported. Shalmaneser defeated Marduk-bêl-usâte, 852 B.C., and in 851 B.C. slew him in battle. Marduk-zâkir-shum became a vassal king. Shalmaneser visited the shrines at Babylon, Borsippa and Kutha, and made rich offerings to the gods. He then subjugated the southern kingdom of Chaldæa. This reign lasted at least eleven years.

MARDUK-BALATSU-IKBI, the son of Marduk-zâkir-shum, followed. He fought with Shamshi-Adad VII. and was defeated with great slaughter at Dûr-Papsukhal. The Babylonians brought a great army of Chaldæans, Aramæans, as well as Elamites, and men from Namri. Again, in 813 B.C., Shamshi-Adad invaded Chaldæa and once more attacked Babylon, but it is not clear who was then on the throne in Babylonia.

An interregnum followed, according to Chronicle K. Probably it only lasted two years.

Then ERBA-MARDUK, son of Marduk-zâkir-shum, came to the throne, and in the second year took the hands of Bêl and so became legitimate king. In the disturbance and confusion the Aramæans had seized upon the fields of the inhabitants of Babylon and Borsippa. Now Erba-Marduk smote them with the sword, took the fields and gardens from them, and restored them to their owners. He set up the throne of Bêl in Êsagila and Ê-zida in the same year. Later, he went to Babylon himself. When Merodach baladan III. came to the throne long after, he claimed to be a descendant of Erba-Marduk.

BAU-AKHI-IDDIN came to the throne next. Adad-nirari IV. made expeditions into Babylonia in 812 B.C., his accession year. In 803 B.C. he went to Chaldæa, and in both 796 B.C. and 795 B.C. to Babylonia. It is difficult to say in which of these expeditions occurred the events recorded by the Synchronous History, which does not name the Assyrian king who shut up Bau-akhi-iddin in his city, captured him, and carried him, with his palace treasures, to Assyria. Dûr-ilu, Lakhiru, Gananâti, Dûr-Pap-sukal, Bît-ridûti, Mê-Turnat, the great cities of Karduniash, with their fortresses, their gods and spoils, were taken. The king went to Kutha, Babylon, and Borsippa, and there offered in token of his supremacy. Then he went down to Chaldæa and received the tribute of the kings there. Then once more the boundaries were settled by treaty. After

H

this thorough conquest Adad-nirari relented and restored the captives to their homes, laid taxes upon them, and the peoples of Assyria and Karduniash were at peace together.

Adad-nirari IV. married Sammu-ramat, undoubtedly a Babylonian princess and identical in name with the fabled Semiramis, queen of Babylon. She evidently played a rôle in the empire quite unique, and her monument at Asshur stood with those of the kings.

There is some probability that, after an interval which we cannot yet fill, NABÛ-MUKÎN-ZÊRI came to the throne, and reigned at least four years.

NABÛ-SHUM-ISHKUM II. was probably the king of whose name traces are to be seen on the Kings' List A after a long break. He reigned thirteen years.

With NABÛ-NATSIR, the Nabonassar of the Greeks, we emerge into the clear light of history. With him begins the Ptolemaic Canon, which gives us the list of the later kings of Babylonia in unbroken order. The Babylonian Chronicle B also now begins, the Kings' List is available still, while the monuments and inscriptions are fuller and more numerous than ever. He reigned fourteen years.

In Assyria, Tiglath-pileser IV. came to the throne in the third year of Nabonassar, and at once marched into Akkad, plundered the cities Rabikum and

Khamrânu, and carried off the gods of Shapazza. Shortly after Borsippa rebelled, and Nabonassar attempted to recapture it, apparently without success.

Tiglath-pileser professed as his object the subjugation of the Aramæan tribes, which had settled in Babylonia and now held Sippar and Dûr-kurigalzu. He claimed to be king of the four quarters of the world, as well as king of Sumer and Akkad. Babylon welcomed him, and by offering in the chief cities of Babylonia he asserted his protectorate over Babylonia. He went no farther south than Nippur, and left the Chaldæans to themselves, but he destroyed their advanced post at Bît-Shilani, and impaled its king, Nabû-ushabshi, before the gate of his destroyed capital, Sarrabanu. He also subdued the Rashâni and Bît-Amukkani.

NABÛ-NÂDIN-ZÊRI, his son, whose name appears in the Babylonian Chronicle as Nadinu and in the Ptolemaic Canon as Nadios, was killed in an insurrection after two years' reign.

The promoter of the rebellion, NABÛ-SHUM-UKÎN II., took the throne, but only ruled for two months. The Babylonian Chronicle calls him Shum-ukîn ; the Kings' List gives him only one month and twelve days.

# CHAPTER IX

## The Ninth Dynasty

THE members of this so-called dynasty really form a collection of disconnected rulers, usurpers, or conquerors. The Kings' List A describes Ukîn-zêr as of the Dynasty of Shashî; Pûlu and Elulai as of Tinu; Marduk-aplu-iddina, Sargon and Sennacherib as Khabigal, which may mean "great robbers." They were certainly not all of the same family.

The Kings' List A places first UKÎN-ZÊR, of the Dynasty of Shashî, with a reign of three years. The Babylonian Chronicle B records that in his third year Tiglath-pileser IV. came down and plundered Bît-Amukâni and captured Ukîn-zêr.

The Kings' List A next gives to Tiglath-pileser IV., the king of Assyria, a reign of two years under the name of PÛLU, the Biblical Pul, the Pôros of the Ptolemaic Canon, which regards him as real ruler along with Ukîn-zêr (Chinzêros) for five years. The Babylonian Chronicle gives Tiglath-pileser two years, before he died in the month of Tebet.

Shalmaneser V., king of Assyria, succeeded, under the name of ULULAI, and reigned as legitimate king for five years.

*PLATE VIII*

**Kudurru of Merodach Baladan III**

We do not know exactly what led to the change
of dynasty in Assyria, but when Sargon ascended
the throne in Tebet, 722 B.C., MERODACH BALADAN
III., the Chaldæan king of Bît Iakîn in the Sealand,
who had once paid tribute to Tiglath-pileser in
729 B.C., seized the throne of Babylon.  He allied
himself with Khumbanigash, king of Elam, and
when Sargon moved south with a hastily organised
army to make good his claim to Shalmaneser's
Empire, the allies made a stout resistance.  Sargon
laid waste Babylonia and brought his enemy to
bay at Dûr-ilu.  Both sides claimed the victory,
but Sargon was obliged to leave Merodach Baladan
in possession of Babylon.  There he reigned un-
disturbed for twelve years, while Sargon held
Dûr-ilu and the cities of Akkad.

Merodach Baladan III., 721-710 B.C.  His rule
was by no means a happy time for Babylonia.
The Chaldæan and Aramæan troops had to be
rewarded with grants of land and property, made
at the expense of native owners.  Merodach Baladan
ruled as a foreign tyrant, and when Sargon was
once more free to try conclusions with him he made
no attempt to hold the capital, but fled south, carrying with him the chief men of Babylon, Borsippa,
Sippar and Nippur as hostages.  Sargon moved
down the east with his resistless army of veterans,
trained in many a fierce war with Armenia and

the west, screened off the Elamites and Aramæans,
subdued the Gambulu, Ru'a, Khindani, Iatburu and
Puqudu, making them into a new province, with
Dûr-Nabû as capital. He then moved into Babylonia and subdued the Aramæan Bît Dakkuri.
Babylonia welcomed the deliverer with joy. The
priests and nobles made a procession to Dûr-
Ladinnu to escort him in triumph into Babylon,
where he offered royal sacrifices. He restored
order in Borsippa, expelling the intruders, took
the hands of Bêl on New Year's Day, 709 B.C.,
becoming legitimate king of Babylon. Then he
turned his attention to Merodach Baladan, who
made an ineffectual stand at Iatburu, was defeated,
and retreated to Iqbi-Bêl, where he was again
defeated, and took refuge in his ancestral capital
of Bît Iakîn, which he fortified against Sargon.
He broke down all the bridges and flooded the
country, but Sargon found a way to penetrate his
defences and laid siege to his capital. Merodach
Baladan now took refuge in Elam. The army of
Puqudu and Sutu, coming to his assistance, were
overpowered, and Bît Iakîn was stormed, sacked
and razed to the ground. Sargon rescued the
Babylonian hostages and restored to them their
possessions. From Chronicle K we learn that
Merodach Baladan's father was Nabû-shum-(ukîn?),
and he claimed descent from Erba-Marduk. His

embassy to Hezekiah of Judah may have been intended to stir up trouble behind Sargon's back, but may more probably have been part of his later intrigues against Sennacherib.

SARGON was now king of Babylonia, 710-704 B.C. He entered upon a series of restorations of temples, city walls, cults of the gods, etc., in Ur, Erech, Eridu and Larsa. Bît Iakîn was stripped of its people, who were deported to Commagene, while the people of that district were settled in their place. Then Bît Iakîn was made an Assyrian province and annexed to Gambuli. Uperi, king of far-off Dilmun, accordingly thought it wise to send presents.

There was a tradition among the Greeks that Sargon made his son, a brother of SENNACHERIB, king of Babylon. Sennacherib himself seems to have been in command on the borders of Armenia when Sargon met a violent death. The Babylonian Chronicle assigns 704 and 703 B.C. to Sennacherib. He did not, however, take the hands of Marduk, and the Ptolemaic Canon, following local opinion, calls these years " kingless." Sennacherib did not at once interfere in Babylonia. According to the Kings' List A, the son of a slave reigned one month, being raised to the throne by a rebellion in which Sennacherib's brother may have fallen. Merodach Baladan again seized the throne, and reigned nine months according to the Kings' List A, six months according to the Babylonian Chronicle. Sennacherib moved across the Tigris, met Merodach Baladan at Kish and utterly routed him. Sennacherib entered Babylon without serious opposition, and sacked Merodach Baladan's palace. He then laid Chaldæa waste, boasting that he had destroyed eighty-nine cities and 820 villages. Merodach Baladan took refuge in Guzuman. Sennacherib sent a vast booty and 208,000 captives to Assyria, leaving behind him Bêl-ibni as a vassal king.

BÊL-IBNI was a native Babylonian prince, brought up at the Assyrian Court, and Sennacherib doubtless thought he would be at once acceptable to the Babylonian people and faithful to Assyria. The experiment answered well for a time, but personal ambition, or the intrigues of the restless nobles, prompted rebellion. In his third year he laid claim to the imperial title of *shar kishshati*, and allied himself with the Chaldæans. Sennacherib carried him off to Assyria after a nominal reign of three years, 700 B.C. His Chaldæan ally, Mushêzib-Marduk, deserted him and took refuge in inaccessible marshes. Merodach Baladan, who had assisted, was attacked, but fled to the West Coast of Elam, embarking his gods and people on ships. There he soon died, while his land of Bît Iakîn was utterly ravaged.

ASHUR-NÂDIN-SHUM, Crown Prince of Assyria, was set on the throne, and reigned six years. Sennacherib now set to work to break the power of the Sealand. He built a fleet and floated it down to the mouth of the rivers, crossed to the Chaldæan settlements in Elam, and there ravaged them, while he himself halted with his army on the mainland. He thus violated Elamite territory, and the king of Elam marched into Babylonia, plundered Sippar, and carried Ashur-nâdin-shum captive to Elam, where he seems to have died. The Elamites and their allies now placed a Chaldæan, Nergal-ushêzib, on the throne, and, supported by his allies, he moved south to attack the Assyrian army in the rear, 693 B.C. Sennacherib retreated to Erech and awaited Nergal-ushêzib, who had taken Nippur. A desperate battle took place, the allies were defeated, and Nergal-ushêzib carried captive to Assyria.

MUSHÊZIB-MARDUK was next raised to the throne, 692 B.C. He was a Chaldæan whom Sennacherib had formerly defeated. Sennacherib took the opportunity afforded by a rebellion in Elam to invade the country in the hope of rescuing his son, but the Elamites retreated to the mountains, and he was beaten back by the cold, 692 B.C. He then attacked Mushêzib-Marduk, who opened the treasuries of Êsagil to bribe the king of Elam to help him, and a great alliance of Elamites, Chaldæans, Aramæans and Babylonians, among them men from Parsua (Persia), Ellipi, Puqudu, Gambuli, with Samunu, son of Merodach Baladan, barred Sennacherib's return at Khalulê, on the east of the Tigris, 691 B.C. He had never been in such peril before. A terrific battle ensued, and Sennacherib claimed the victory. At any rate he got through to Assyria, but left Mushêzib-Marduk alone for the time.

In 689 B.C. SENNACHERIB had recovered and came again. Elam held aloof. Babylon was taken, and Mushêzib-Marduk sent in chains to Assyria. Sennacherib then set to work to obliterate Babylon. The whole city was sacked, fortifications and walls, temples and palaces, as well as private houses, were levelled with the ground, the people massacred or deported, and the waters of the Arakhtu canal turned over the site. Mushêzib-Marduk's reign had lasted one year and six months at most.

Sennacherib himself may now be said to have reigned seven years over Babylon. But as he had carried away Marduk to Assyria, he could not take the hands of Bêl, and so could not be legitimate king. The Babylonian Chronicle and Ptolemaic Canon call these eight years " kingless." Berosus seems to have given a rule of eight years here to Axerdis, possibly intending Esarhaddon by that name. Babylonia was made an Assyrian province under a viceroy.

Doubtless the scattered population soon began to drift back to Babylon, and there is reason to think that ESARHADDON ruled there as "Vice-regent of Bêl" before his father's death, and began to restore the city. He was probably there when Sennacherib was murdered, 20th Tebet, 681 B.C., and marched thence to wrest Assyria from his brother, Ashur-shar-etir, the Biblical Sharezer. After he ascended the throne of Assyria, 680 B.C., Babylon remained under his rule. But as the statue of Marduk remained captive in Assyria, he could not be real king, and only retained the title of Viceroy. During his frequent absences warring in the west, his mother, Naqia, was regent, and the Elamites saw an opening to raid Babylonia and capture Sippar. In the south, Nabû-zêru-kênish-lishir, a son of Merodach Baladan, possessed himself of the Sealand and captured Ur. The Assyrian generals drove back both invasions. Nabû-zêru-kênish-lishir was defeated and fled to Elam, where he was slain. His brother, Nâ'id-Marduk surrendered to Esarhaddon, who made him vassal king of the Sealand. Esarhaddon drove out the Chaldæans, who had again settled in Babylonia, subdued the Gambuli, and set up their king, Bêl-ikisha, in Shapi-Bêl as a frontier post against Elam ; deposed Shamash-erba, the king of Bît Dakkuri, and set up Nabû-usallim, son of that Balasu whom

Tiglath-pileser had fought. The Elamite king
made peace and returned the gods he had carried
off. Esarhaddon greatly favoured Babylon, and
rebuilt large portions of it. All over Babylonia he
restored city walls, temples, cults and canals.
Under him Babylon would soon have recovered.
He died 668 B.C.

Esarhaddon left Assyria to his son, Ashur-banipal,
and Babylon to his son, SHAMASH-SHUM-UKÎN. After
partaking in the coronation of his brother, Shamash-
shum-ukîn brought back the statue of Marduk to
Babylon, Aiaru, 668 B.C., and on the New Year's
Day of 667 B.C. took the hands of Bêl and became
legitimate king of Babylon and Amnanu. Ashur-
banipal retained the rule of all the south and continued to offer royal sacrifices in Babylon, Borsippa,
Sippar and Kutha, as overlord. The southern
cities were under Assyrian governors. At first
Shamash-shum-ukîn turned his mind to works of
peace, fortifications and restorations. His brother
gave him ample Assyrian troops as guards against
Elam. But as he felt himself grow stronger he
began to make a bid for independence. He drew
into a conspiracy against his brother, Ummanigash,
king of Elam, Arabians, Aramæans, Chaldæans,
Egypt, Ethiopia and Gutium. When the affair
seemed ripe he sent a challenge to Ashur-banipal
forbidding him any longer to offer sacrifices in

Babylonian cities. He then seized Ur and Erech. Ashur-banipal moved with great deliberation, but after a decisive victory at Bâb-Samî, in Arakhsamna, 650 B.C., he laid siege to Borsippa, Babylon, Kutha and Sippara, and leaving his armies to blockade them, rapidly reduced the South. Babylon stood a siege from Arakhsamna, 650 B.C., to Aiaru 648 B.C. Soon after it was stormed, after suffering the last extremities of famine and pestilence. It was then sacked as ruthlessly as by Sennacherib, and everything given over to fire and massacre. Shamash-shum-ukîn burnt himself to death in his palace.

Borsippa held out a little longer, Sippar and Kutha had fallen earlier. They were treated better, and Babylon was handed over to them to settle in. Shamash-shum-ukîn had reigned twenty years.

Ashur-banipal henceforth ruled Babylonia himself. KANDALANU, the Kineladanus of Ptolemy, whom Berosus calls brother of Sammuges, was either a throne name of Ashur-banipal's or of his nominee. He reigned twenty years.

When Ashur-banipal died, 628 B.C., Babylon itself fell into the hands of Nabopolassar, who founded the New Babylonian Empire. Ashur-etil-ilâni and Sin-shar-ishkun, the sons of Ashur-banipal, and kings of Assyria, retained possession of the cities of Akkad and the South, such as Nippur, Ur and Erech, for some time.

# CHAPTER X

## The Tenth Dynasty, or Neo-Babylonian Empire

Nabopolassar reigned from 625 to 604 b.c. His rule was very limited at first. For four years we have no proof that his rule was acknowledged beyond Babylon and Borsippa. Erech, Nippur and even Sippara remained under Assyrian rule for much longer.

He allied himself with the king of the Medes, who devastated Mesopotamia and ultimately captured Nineveh which fell towards the end of his reign, about 606 b.c. He boasts that he had chased from Akkad the Assyrians " who from days of old had ruled over all peoples and worn out the nations with their heavy yoke." He further claims to have " laid the foundation " of his land and rule.

His many inscriptions are chiefly concerned with his buildings. He was a great restorer. He rebuilt the great temple of Marduk at Babylon, while he had not yet assumed the title of king of Babylon, though already claiming to be king of Sumer and Akkad. When he dug a canal at Sippara, where he also built a temple of Bêlit, he claims to be king of Babylon.  He fortified Babylon, with its inner wall called Imgur-Marduk.

On the fall of Nineveh, Pharaoh Necho II., king of Egypt, in 609 B.C., made an attempt to revive Egyptian supremacy.  The Egyptians had already reached the Euphrates, when Nabopolassar's army, under his son, Nebuchadrezzar, met and defeated them at Carchemish, 605 B.C.  A Babylonian settlement of the West was in progress when Nabopolassar died, and Nebuchadrezzar hastened back across the desert from Pelusium, on the borders of Egypt, to claim the throne of Babylon.

NEBUCHADREZZAR II. reigned from 604 B.C. to 561 B.C.  His own inscriptions, like his father's, deal almost solely with buildings.  He fortified Babylon with an outer wall, Nimitti-Bêl, and with moats ; he made the great city gates of cedar, covered with strips of decorated bronze.  Outside this he ultimately constructed fortifications so extended that no army could have surrounded it.  Within, he built a citadel palace, and made magnificent streets.  He cleaned out the Arakhtu canal, which ran through Babylon, and lined it with quays.  The Babylon with its hanging gardens, once the wonder of the world, was practically his creation, and is the immense city whose ruins the Germans are now exploring.

Nebuchadrezzar prided himself on the restoration

of the ancient temples of his land. At Sippara, Larsa, Ur, Dilbat, Baz, Erech, Borsippa, Kutha, Marad, and many another less celebrated place, he lavished his wealth upon his gods and their dwellings. Nor did he care less for the well-being of his people. He cleared out the old canals and dug a new one north of Sippara.

Nebuchadrezzar was undoubtedly a great warrior, and fully maintained the prestige won by the armies of Assyria in the West, but only a tiny fragment of his annals has survived. They record that in his thirty-seventh year he warred in Egypt against Amasis, and a reference to Phut and Iaman probably indicates his victory over the Egyptian allies and Greek mercenaries. Josephus preserves a tradition that he made Egypt a Babylonian province. From the same source we learn of his siege of Tyre, 585 to 573 B.C. Tyre finally made terms under Ethobaal, but was never captured.

From the Biblical records we learn a full account of his relations with Judæa, some details of which still elude our grasp, but the questions involved belong rather to the treatment of the Old Testament than to a history of Babylonia. Traces of his wars in the West, which were by no means confined to Judah, are to be found in a much mutilated inscription on the rocks at Wady Brissa, a valley north of the Lebanon mountains, and west of the upper part of the Orontes, and in an inscription and image set up at the Nahr-el-kelb.

AMÊL-MARDUK, 561-560 B.C., the Biblical Evil-Merodach, son of Nebuchadrezzar, only reigned two years and a few months. According to the Biblical accounts he had compassion on Jehoiachin, the captive Jewish king, taking him out of prison and making him an honoured, though compulsory, guest.

According to the story quoted from Berosus, he had rendered himself so hateful by his debaucheries and extravagance that he was assassinated.

NERIGLISSAR, Nergal-shar-utsur, probably the Nergal-shar-ezer who was Rabmag at the siege of Jerusalem, brother-in-law of Amêl-Marduk, was son of Bêl-shum-ishkun, and had married a daughter of Nebuchadrezzar. His own inscriptions deal almost entirely with temple buildings at Babylon and Borsippa, where he built himself a palace, 559-556 B.C.

LABASHI-MARDUK, his son, the Labarosoarchod of Berosus, is said by him to have been lawless and impious, and was deposed by the priestly party, who set Nabonidus on the throne, 556 B.C. He reigned only nine months, and was but a child.

NABONIDUS, Nabû-nâ'id, son of Nabû-balatsu-iqbi, 556-540 B.C., a native Babylonian, was its last independent king. He was, above all, a restorer of

I

temples. It was his great delight to search for the
foundation records of the original founders, and he
prided himself on retaining, to a finger-breadth, the
former dimensions of their buildings. To him more
than to anyone else we are indebted for references
to early history, which enable us to reconstruct
chronology.

His list of restorations is very long. Everywhere calling himself the preserver of Êsagila in
Babylon and Ê-zida at Borsippa, his greatest achievement was the rebuilding of the temple of Shamash
at Sippara on a scale of magnificence previously
unrivalled. For its roof alone five thousand beams
of cedar were employed. In the city of Sippar of
Anunîtum her temple, Ê-ulmash, was restored.

From an inscription drawn up to commemorate
his restoration of the temple of Sin at Haran, we
learn that in his sixth year one Cyrus, son of Cam-
byses, king of Anshan, a petty vassal of Astyages,
king of the Medes, " with his small army " conquered
that powerful monarch. This led to the with-
drawal of the Manda from Haran, where Nabonidus had long wished to restore the temple. It
had been destroyed by the Manda, probably in
concert with the Babylonians, as the statues of
its gods had been preserved in Babylon. Ashur-
banipal had rebuilt the temple on the foundations
laid by Shalmaneser, 859-825 B.C. Nabonidus

again rebuilt it with greater splendour than ever.
He enumerates with pride the countries which
owned his sway, Babylonia, all Mesopotamia and
the Western lands down to Gaza, on the borders of
Egypt. Governors, princes, and kings united to
contribute to the grand work.

CYRUS soon made himself master of the Median
Empire, and a coalition was formed against him
by Crœsus, king of Lydia, Amasis, king of Egypt,
and Nabonidus, king of Babylonia. On the fall of
Crœsus in 546 B.C., Cyrus turned his attention to
Nabonidus, who had estranged the powerful priesthood of Marduk at Babylon by his devotion to the
worship of Sin at Haran and Ur, and of Shamash at
Sippara and Larsa. A Chronicle dealing with the
events of this reign once had entries for each year.
It was drawn up by a priest of Êsagila, and reflects
the dissatisfaction there by its perpetually recurring
notice, " the king was in Tema so Bêl went not
forth." As the king was not present on the New
Year's festival to take the hands of Marduk, that
god could not make his procession. On the part
of Nabonidus this was equivalent to abdicating his
claim to be legitimate king in the metropolis of
the Empire. Where Tema was and what hold it
had upon Nabonidus we do not know. He seems
to have left affairs of state and the command of
the army to his beloved son, Belshazzar, for whom

he perpetually records his prayer for safety and preservation from sin against the gods.

The end soon came, for the defence was entrusted to Belshazzar, who lay with his army in Akkad, but was signally defeated at Opis, and, on the 14th of Tammuz, Sippara fell without fighting. On the 16th, Gobryas entered Babylon without resistance, and Cyrus followed on the 3rd of Marchesvan 539-8 B.C. He was received openly by all classes as a liberator. Nabonidus was exiled to Carmania.

A monument found near Haran contains an autobiography of the father of Nabonidus, who was possibly installed there as priest of Sin towards the end of Ashur-banipal's reign. He mentions that king, his son Ashur-etil-ilâni, Nabopolassar, Nebuchadrezzar, and Nergalsharutsur, for whom he regularly prayed, and reckons 104 years of life from the days of Ashur-banipal to the sixth year of Nabonidus. In this year took place the death of the mother of Nabonidus at Dûr-kurasu, near Sippara, on the 5th of Nisan.

---

### NOTE ON THE DYNASTY OF GUTIUM (p. 46).

A newly found inscription shows that the men of Gutium were finally expelled from Babylonia by Utu-khegal, who captured their king, Tirigam, and founded a dynasty at Erech, which must have preceded that of Ur.

# BIBLIOGRAPHY

GOODSPEED, G. S. *A History of the Babylonians and Assyrians.* London: Smith, Elder & Co. 1903.

KING, L. W. *A History of Sumer and Akkad.* London: Chatto & Windus. 1910.

THUREAU-DANGIN, F. *Die sumerischen und akkadischen Königsinschriften.* Leipzig: Hinrichs. 1907.

HINKE, W. J. *A New Boundary Stone of Nebuchadrezzar I.* Philadelphia: University of Pennsylvania. 1907.

LANGDON, S. *Die neubabylonischen Königsinschriften.* Leipzig: Hinrichs. 1912.

SCHNABEL, P. *Studien zur babylonischen-assyrischen Chronologie.* Berlin: W. Peiser. 1908.

HOGG, H. W. *The Isin Dynasty.* Manchester: Journal Manchester Oriental Society. 1912.

Numerous articles in the *Orientalistische Litteratur-Zeitung, Revue d'Assyriologie, Zeitschrift für Assyriologie, Proceedings of the Society of Biblical Archæology,* and other periodicals deal at length with the subjects summarised in this book, and give references to original sources.

# INDEX

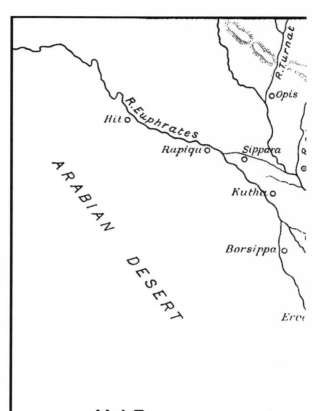

MAP
OF
BABYLONIA

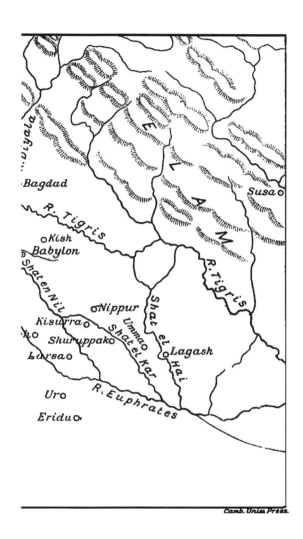

www.ingramcontent.com/pod-product-compliance
Ingram Content Group UK Ltd.
Pitfield, Milton Keynes, MK11 3LW, UK
UKHW042144280225
455719UK00001B/84

9 781107 605725